Face to Face: A Guide for Supervisors Who Counsel Problem Employees

by

James M. Carroll

Published by:
FPMI Communications, Inc. • 707 Fiber St.
Huntsville, AL 35801-5833
(256) 539-1850 • Fax: (256) 539-0911

Internet Address:
http://www.fpmi.com • e-mail: fpmi@fpmi.com

© 1999 by FPMI Communications, Inc. ISBN 0-936295-75-9

All rights reserved. No part of this publication may be reproduced, stored in a retrieval system, or transmitted, in any form or by any means, electronic, mechanical, photocopying, recording, or otherwise, without the written permission of the publisher.

JAMES M. CARROLL

Jim Carroll has been advising federal government supervisors for 26 years, both as an employee of the government and as a private consultant. He has taught hundreds of courses on supervision, with particular emphasis on dealing with problem employees. He has advised managers on disciplinary and performance based actions, and has defended agency actions before the Merit Systems Protection Board and in arbitration.

Jim conducts seminars for FPMI Communications on a range of labor and employee relations issues.

ACKNOWLEDGEMENTS

In preparing this book, I turned to some friends who I knew would not hesitate to tell me where I had gone wrong. Their numerous criticisms and ideas were invaluable. They are: Vicki Braun, Bill Fleming, Mary Fleming, Ron Garland, Dwight Holman, Chris Kunz, Kathi McDaniel, Nancy Palmer, Gary Silver, Dean Teasdale, Mike Tolle and Gene Vanek.

Finally, I want to thank Marilyn Dickman, my closest friend, whose advice gets me through just about everything I do.

FPMI COMMUNICATIONS

TABLE OF CONTENTS

FPMI
COMMUNICATIONS

NOTE:

Because of the nature of the subject, the vast majority of this book is applicable to supervisors at all levels of government. We have noted those sections which are federal-specific directly in the text.

INTRODUCTION AND DEFINITION

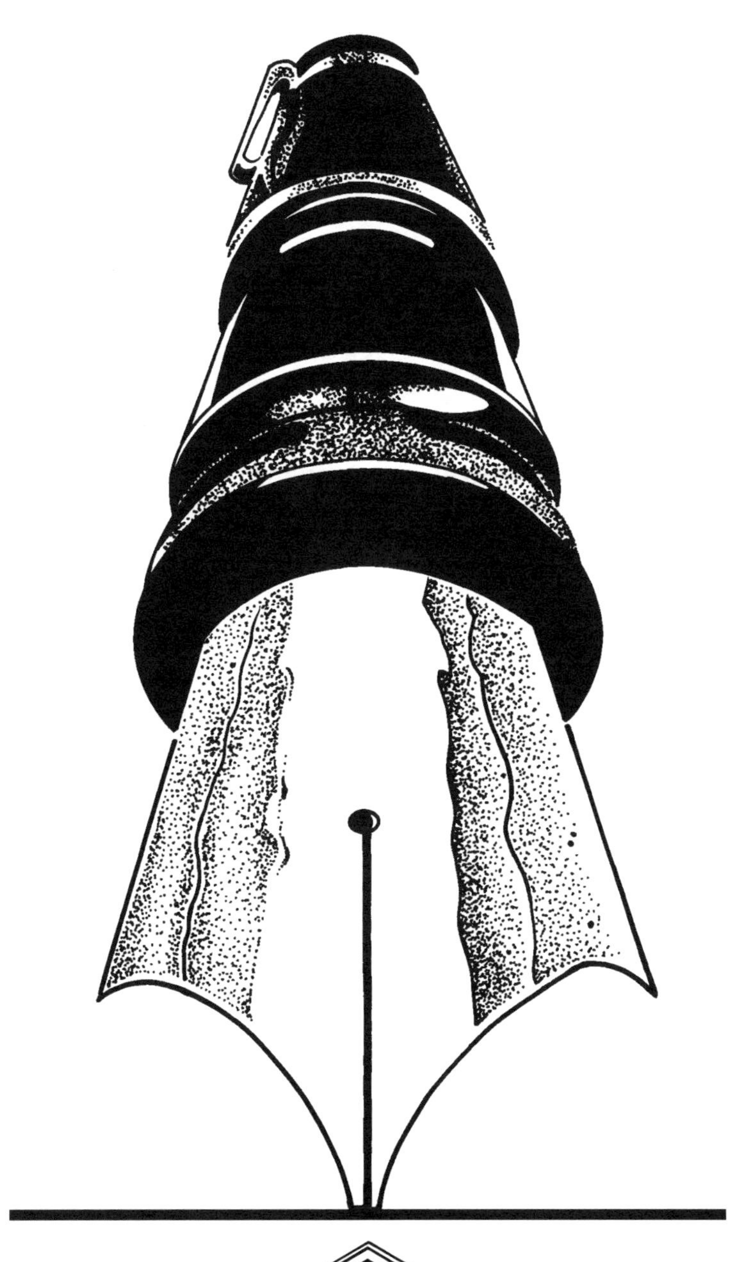

Face To Face

Counseling employees who are having problems at work is the hardest part of a supervisor's job.

Supervision is probably the most difficult job there is, whether you supervise research scientists, clerks or mechanics. Counseling employees who are having problems at work is the hardest part of the supervisor's job. Sometimes it seems hardly a day goes by that you don't have to talk to someone about something unpleasant.

Certainly, supervision has its share of pleasant experiences. Giving someone a well deserved outstanding performance rating, or handing out a cash award to a hard working employee are the types of things that make your day. But this book is not about the fun part of being a supervisor. Rather, it is about those things supervisors dread. Very few supervisors relish the chore of telling someone his performance must improve. No one looks forward to talking to an employee about her use of sick leave.

The best supervisors are those who are able to deal with confrontation and handle the people aspect of the job.

Supervisors have a lot to do. The textbooks on supervision and management often refer to management functions: planning, organizing, controlling, etc. However important these functions are, no matter how vital to a supervisor's success, the best supervisors are those who are able to deal with confrontation. The best planners and the best organizers are useless to an organization if they can't successfully handle the people aspects of the job. This is more true today than it has ever been. Employees and their representatives are more aggressive in pursuing what they believe are employee rights, and they are less fearful of adverse consequences.

Supervisors are becoming increasingly reluctant to confront poor performance or misconduct, as they fear the inevitable complaints that will follow. However, everyone knows that problems only continue to grow if they are not handled early. Unfortunately, problems not only grow; they spread. If you do not deal with a poorly performing employee, his performance gets worse, as might be expected. But in today's workplace, the performance of his coworkers is also likely to decline. People know what's going on. They know who is carrying his share of the workload and who isn't. They may not come right out and say it, but they expect you to handle those who aren't doing the job. If you don't, you can expect to face an attitude that says, *"Why should I do a good job, if others don't have to?"*

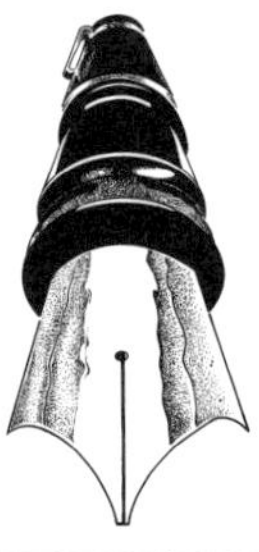

The problem is not in figuring out <u>when</u> to counsel, but <u>how</u> to do it.

A management trainer once had a call from a high level manager in a military organization, who asked if he could give his supervisors some training on *when* to counsel employees. The trainer's response was that supervisors don't need training on *when* to counsel. That's the easy part. Anyone with any sense knows when an employee has begun to go astray. The problem is not figuring out *when* to do it. The problem is *how* to do it. What do you say? How is the employee going to respond? How do you respond to that? What are the legal issues involved? What if she brings a representative? Is she entitled to do so? What if the employee or representative is more experienced than you at confrontation?

These are the kinds of questions that will be addressed in this book. The purpose is to give you practical ways to approach workplace confrontations. This book will not make you a psychology expert or a professional counselor. Rather, this book will give you tips on how to handle specific situations supervisors can expect to face. It will explore how to plan for confrontations, and how to achieve your own objectives. It will not address every possible problem. Given the many characters who make up the workforce, that would be impossible. We will deal here with the more typical things that happen at work. Bizarre people and situations will be left for the psychology texts.

The book is written specifically for supervisors of government employees. Anyone who has ever attempted to do so knows that supervising under the federal, or other public personnel system is a unique experience. Employees enjoy more protections than can be found in most other personnel systems. Armed with these many protections, particularly prohibitions against retaliation for filing complaints, employees feel free to say what they want when speaking with their supervisors. They are more prone to make use of the numerous appeal and grievance procedures available to them. This is not an attempt to make you run and hide from confrontations. Rather, the purpose is to encourage you to be better prepared to deal with the inevitable situations that will arise.

Solving the problem is the ultimate outcome of every counseling.

In the chapters ahead, we will deal with confrontations that you initiate, specifically, counseling meetings with employees. The emphasis will be on the practical aspects of counseling, how to plan for it, what to say and what to avoid. However, recognizing the complexities of the federal system, we will have to take an occasional look at the legal aspects, and review the rights and responsibilities of both supervisors and employees when confrontations occur.

This book is not about winning and losing. It does not advocate trickery or deception. However, it is written for the supervisor. Its purpose is to help supervisors do a better job, and achieve their objectives. Given this focus, it may at times come across as adversarial. Some of the techniques suggested may appear harsh. In today's workplace, supervisors often go into counseling meetings with the feeling that they are responsible for fixing all problems. They face representatives who are knowledgeable and experienced, and they face employees who know their rights. The purpose is to give supervisors some tools that will be useful to place the responsibility where it belongs and solve the problem at hand, while maintaining some balance in the discussions. You are expected to handle performance and conduct problems when necessary, but every word you say is subject to challenge. You have a right to expect to be backed up by your superiors, but to deserve such support, you must do it right. Solving the problem is the ultimate outcome of every counseling.

Don't expect counseling to be pleasant.

You probably have already noticed that the terms *counseling* and *confrontation* are used interchangeably in this book. While this may not be a popular approach with some experts, it is done quite consciously. When you make the decision to talk with an employee about a behavior or performance problem, you have decided it is time to confront a situation. Don't expect it to be pleasant. You are not going to war with that employee, but you should not expect, nor attempt, to make the process a pleasant experience. Those supervisors who go out of their way to be non-confrontational in their counseling efforts often fail to get the message across. They make many of the mistakes that are described in the pages that follow.

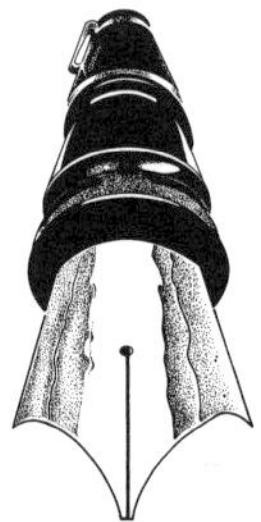

What Do We Mean By Counseling?

For the purposes of this book, we will define counseling as follows.

> *Counseling is a process occurring between a supervisor and an employee, that has as its objective some positive change in the employee's behavior or performance.*

Each word or phrase in the definition is very important.

Counseling is a process...

Many, if not most employees with problems will need more than one meeting to resolve the problem.

Sometimes, if you are very lucky, a problem can be overcome in just one meeting. Some employees merely have to be told once that a certain behavior is not acceptable, or that a specific work product did not meet your standard, and that will be the end of it. The situation will not happen again. Believe it or not, there are some employees out there who consider themselves *testers.* These people believe it is their responsibility to determine, both for themselves and their co-workers, which rules management is serious about enforcing. The only way to do this is to occasionally break a rule and watch for the supervisor's reaction. If the supervisor counsels the tester, the rule is still in effect. If not, the word goes out to all employees that they are free to ignore that rule. The tester wants to be counseled. One warning usually resolves the issue, at least for a while.

Unfortunately, you will not be this lucky very often. Many, if not most employees with behavior or performance problems will need more than one meeting before the problem is resolved. This is particularly true in dealing with performance deficiencies. As you will see in a later chapter, employees who truly want to perform well, but lack some skill or ability, will need several counseling sessions before you can expect to see some performance improvement. Employees who engage in misconduct are easier to deal with than non-performers, but even they may need occasional reminders after the initial counseling session.

The only way to insure that you get a lasting change is to stay on top of the situation.

The point is, a supervisor cannot view counseling as a one time occurrence. Some supervisors are so happy to get a counseling session done, they actually avoid the employee for months. If you don't get the change in the employee that motivated you to do the counseling, you've wasted your time. The only way to ensure that you get a lasting change is to stay on top of the situation. After a counseling session, the employee must be carefully observed, in order to see if any change is taking place. If it is, the employee should be told so, in order to keep things moving in the right direction. If the expected change is not happening, more counseling might be in order.

Between a supervisor and an employee...

Hopefully, most counseling will be a one on one experience between these two parties. However, there may be times when the employee will seek to have a representative present. There also may be times when the situation is so volatile, the supervisor will want to have another management official in the room. These are the unusual occurrences, and will be dealt with in later chapters. For now, we will view counseling as a process in which the supervisor identifies the need for some change, communicates that need to the employee, and the two work together in a good faith effort to bring about the desired change. It won't always be that smooth, but you must begin the process by viewing it as a one on one experience. Your goal is to bring about the change without making a federal case of it.

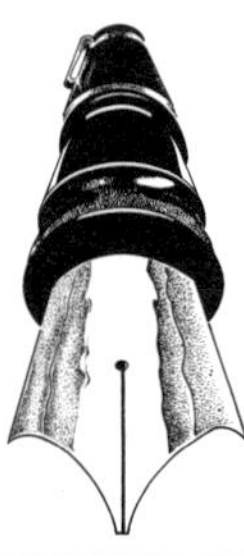

Some supervisors worry so much about the counsel-ing process, they forget about the purpose.

That has as its objective...

The word *objective* is key here. Some supervisors worry so much about the counseling session itself, they forget about the purpose. Not only should there be an objective for the counseling process, there ought to be a separate objective for every counseling meeting. Without objectives, there can be no plan. Without a plan, the supervisor lacks control of the counseling process, and often finds herself on the defensive. In a later chapter, we will spend some time on developing a *meeting objective,* that is, an objective for each distinct counseling session. It may seem like a lot of extra work at first, but it doesn't take much, and it really helps you to keep the counseling session on track.

Some positive change...

This part of our definition obviously overlooks an important aspect of employee counseling. You should also counsel employees in order to maintain a certain level of performance, or to reinforce certain behaviors. This is positive counseling, and it is easy to do, although some would say it's not done enough. If you make it a practice to reinforce good performance or behavior with employees, the other type of counseling, designed to bring about change, will be easier.

Reinforce good performance or behavior.

As mentioned in the Introduction, this book is about the difficult part of supervision. So, we will not spend time on positive counseling. Our purpose is to deal with counseling when a problem has been observed. But we would be negligent if we didn't at least mention the importance of positive counseling.

In the employee's behavior or performance.

Depending on the employee's problem, different techniques should be used in the counseling process.

This aspect of our definition is important. There are many skilled, competent employees who don't behave the way you want. That is, they take too many unplanned days off, or disrupt the work of others. Maybe they simply have an uncooperative attitude. We will refer to these people as conduct or behavior problems.

On the other hand, there are many employees who really try hard. They show up on time, get along well with their coworkers, have friendly, cooperative attitudes, but simply lack the knowledge or skill needed to perform acceptably. These people must be treated differently when the supervisor engages in counseling. The causes of their problems are different, and the approach to finding solutions must be different.

Later, we will look at different counseling techniques or approaches, and we will discuss the directive approach and the non-directive approach. When dealing with conduct problems, the directive approach is the best route to take, but the non-directive approach works best with employees having performance difficulties.

A supervisor who is successful at counseling is one who plans, is flexible, and is able to use counseling skills to fit the situation. When dealing with a problem employee the first, and perhaps most important, question you can ask is *"Am I dealing with someone who wants to but can't; or is this someone who just doesn't care?"* A correct answer to that question is a necessary starting point for you to achieve your counseling objectives.

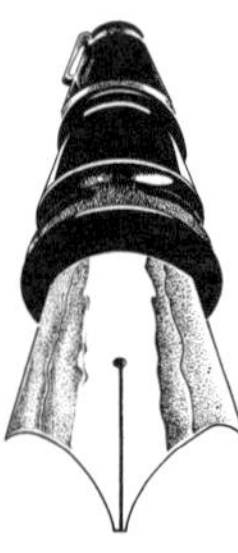

THE OBSTACLES

Chapter 1

The biggest obstacle to effective counseling is fear.

You will find yourself dealing, at times, with employees who don't behave properly. On other occasions, you will have to confront employees who are not performing satisfactorily. These different problems require different counseling skills and approaches. They will be discussed in separate chapters later. In this chapter, we will examine some of the problems you can expect to face no matter which type of problem you are trying to resolve.

Fear

Most supervisors with common sense know when a situation requires counseling. Sick leave patterns are quite obvious. Missed deadlines, or work that must be returned are easily observed. These are the types of situations that cry out for counseling, early, before they become complicated problems. Yet most supervisors avoid dealing with these problems, hoping they will go away. You can always find a reason not to counsel an employee. There's always too much real work to do. Your boss has imposed deadlines that must be met. These are excuses, and every supervisor knows it. The real reason you don't tackle these problems early is simple. You're afraid. You put it off, worry about it and torture yourself over it, not because there's too much other work to do. Admit it. You simply fear sitting down face to face with an employee and telling him you don't like his work, his attendance, his attitude, or whatever it is that's bothering you.

Now that you have recognized the biggest obstacle to effective counseling, consider the following. Even those supervisors who have highly developed counseling skills will tell you they experience the same fear and worry you do as they enter the counseling process. No one likes to tell an employee there is a problem. It simply is not a pleasant experience. If they were honest, most supervisors would admit that the night before a scheduled counseling session they lose sleep. They toss and turn or pace the floor worrying about what they are going to say, how the employee is going to react, and how they will respond to the possible things they might hear the next day.

Even supervisors with highly developed counseling skills experience fear and worry.

It is perfectly normal to feel fear., but problems occur if you don't handle that fear properly.

Here's the bad news. Reading this book may lessen your fear, but it will not rid you of it. You will probably continue to lose sleep over the need to talk to your problem employees. The good news: it's perfectly normal to feel this way. Fearing the counseling process is not a problem. Problems occur if you don't handle your fear properly. If you continue to put it off or make excuses for not talking with the employee, fear has won out. If you go into the counseling session and soften the problem to avoid a negative reaction from the employee, fear has once again prevailed. However, if you use your fear to help develop sound counseling objectives and an effective plan, you've conquered the fear.

Given the fact that you will likely never get over the fear or distaste for counseling, consider this idea as some compensation. Call it the principle of *shared worry.* Go to the employee the day before the counseling meeting, a Friday afternoon is often a good idea. Tell her about the meeting you are planning and its exact purpose. Don't say *"Let's get together and talk Monday."* Instead say *"At ten o'clock Monday morning, I want to meet to discuss your recent use of sick leave."*

Share your worry. Make the people who cause you problems to lose a little sleep too.

The purpose of this approach is to share some of that worry. Supervisors agonize over these problems, sometimes for weeks or months, before they confront the employee. In the meantime, the employee skates happily along, apparently oblivious to the problems he is causing. While you are losing sleep the night before the meeting, shouldn't you take some comfort in the fact that he is also? They don't pay you enough money to carry these burdens by yourself. Share some of it. Make the people who cause you problems lose a little sleep.

Some would argue that this idea is a bad one, because, aside from sharing the worry, it allows the employee time to get ready for the counseling. It eliminates the element of surprise. Why would you want to surprise a problem employee? All that does is allow the person to claim ignorance of the situation, and to prolong the counseling meeting with a lengthy discussion of whether there really is a problem. You want your people prepared for counseling. You want to get

In most cases, the principle of shared worry will work to your advantage.

to the heart of the problem and deal with it. You don't want silly games or expressions of shock and surprise when the employee is being counseled.

The principle of shared worry not only benefits you, it also gives the employee fair notice that he'd better be prepared to discuss the problem. As with just about every other suggestion made in this book, there will be exceptions. There are some people you don't want to notify in advance. These are people who may be unstable and unpredictable. You are the best judge of your employees and their likely reaction. In most cases, the principle of shared worry will work to your advantage. In a few situations, the element of surprise might be more beneficial.

Denial, Disbelief and Ignorance

Often, the employee will express surprise that the supervisor sees a need for counseling. He absolutely will be shocked to hear that you think there is a problem. Don't fall for this one. Ignorance is a common initial defense to counseling. The first thing to recognize is that most problem employees know they are problem employees. They are actually waiting for you to confront them, and they are wondering why it's taking you so long to get around to it. They will never admit this, of course. Often, they won't even admit it to themselves. Denial is a normal human reaction to a person's shortcomings. However, almost any person knows when he's taking too much time off, or when she's not putting out a top quality work product.

You can expect a certain amount of denial or feigned surprise.

There are exceptions. Some people truly believe they are making an outstanding contribution when, in fact, they aren't carrying their weight. These are rare, but they are out there.

No matter which type of employee you are confronting, at the initial counseling meeting, you can expect some denial or feigned surprise. There are two ways to overcome this. First, you must be prepared

Attack problems early.

with facts that prove there is a problem. *"I've noticed you've been taking quite a few long lunches lately"* is not a bad opening statement. However, after the expression of denial, you had better be prepared with something like this. *"On Monday, you were gone for about two hours. Last Thursday, it was an hour and a half. Tuesday, it was two hours..."* This is not to suggest that you follow people around and write down every transgression. But, when you spot a problem, and you know you are going to have to do some counseling, you have to gather facts. If you can't prove there's a reason to confront the employee, you leave yourself open to the ignorance defense.

The other way to avoid denial by the employee is to attack problems early. The longer you let a problem go on, the more right the employee has to claim ignorance. If he has been doing lousy work for a year, and you finally decide to confront the situation, you can expect that he will deny any knowledge of the problem. In his mind, he still knows he has been doing a bad job. But at that counseling meeting, he will use the ignorance excuse to put you immediately on the defensive.

If your objective is to fix a problem, plan on spending considerable time with the employee.

Time

Effective counseling takes a heavy investment of time. The time you will spend counseling problem employees depends on your motivation. If you merely want to counsel so that you can document that counseling occurred, in order to support a later disciplinary action, the amount of time spent can be minimal. However, if your objective is to fix the problem, plan on spending considerable time with the employee. This goes back to our earlier point that counseling is a process, usually not a one time event. There is no way to resolve the time problem, except to try to make your counseling meetings as productive as possible. This can be accomplished with proper planning and preparation, which will be discussed in later chapters. There are no other shortcuts.

Plan and prepare for your counseling meetings. Do not take shortcuts.

Keep this point in mind. You are going to spend the time one way or the other. As the guy in the commercial says, *"Pay me now or pay me later."* If you shortcut the counseling process to save time, you're going to have to keep spending time on the problem that will not go away on its own. If you counsel only to support a disciplinary action, plan on spending lots of time defending yourself in the appeals process.

> As one wise supervisor once said, *"Only about 10 percent of my employees are problems; unfortunately that 10 percent consumes 90 percent of my time."*

Space

Counseling must be a private process. Unfortunately, in government, many supervisors work in cubicles, not in private offices. This can be blamed on some of our modern management gurus who advocate openness in the workplace, as well as our computer wizards who design the new systems furniture configurations. But it's not going to change. So, for counseling purposes, you must work around it. If you have a private office, you're all set. If not, prepare to improvise. You can find a quiet conference room or a corner in the cafeteria. Whatever you do, you must establish a setting in which the two of you are free to raise your voices and get a little emotional, if necessary. If either of you feels stifled, it is going to be more difficult to achieve your objectives.

One manager has a practice of walking around the block with employees he is counseling. This is somewhat effective, but other employees know who is in trouble, if they see their coworker taking a walk with the boss. Most organizations have at least a few private conference rooms where counseling meetings can take place. Again, other employees draw conclusions when they see employee and supervisor using the conference room. Keep in mind, your main objective is privacy, where both parties feel free to speak. The fact that others might perceive an employee is in some trouble is secondary.

You must establish a setting in which the two of you are free to raise your voices, if necessary.

You gain a lot of respect from people when they think you are confronting a problem employee.

Harsh as it may appear, this perception works in the supervisor's favor. You gain a lot of respect from the people when they think you are confronting a problem employee. They already know who the problems are.

Once you have found private space, the physical placement of desks, tables and chairs becomes an issue. There are experts who believe the physical arrangement of the room, including where each party sits, and the barriers between the parties, has an effect on the success of the counseling meeting. There is probably some validity to these theories, although they can be taken to the extreme. Given the limited control government supervisors have over such things, you should try to conduct your counselings in private settings, where the parties are relatively comfortable. Hopefully, there will be desks or tables to allow each of you to take notes. As we will see later, note taking is important for both the supervisor and the employee. So a business setting is preferable to a walk around the block, where taking notes will be difficult.

Finding adequate space is a function of proper planning for the counseling meeting. If you start looking five minutes before the meeting, you are taking a big risk. Unfortunately, many counseling meetings turn into disasters because of a lack of planning.

Representatives

Earlier, we defined counseling as a one on one situation between supervisor and employee. However, we also recognized there would be times when the employee will perceive a need for representation. A request for representation at a counseling meeting raises both legal and practical considerations. We will look first at the legal right to representation enjoyed by federal employees. State and local government organizations will no doubt face similar considerations, but will vary according to state law and the collective bargaining agreement.

Generally, an employee has no right to representation at a counseling meeting.

Generally speaking, an employee has no right to representation at a *counseling* meeting. Federal labor law gives employees the right to union representation at *investigative* meetings. Note that this right extends only to employees who are members of recognized bargaining units. If the purpose of the meeting is to counsel the employee, but not to elicit facts that might be used for disciplinary purposes later, the meeting is not investigative. This would eliminate the legal right to representation at just about any performance discussion. The distinction between counseling and investigation seems simple, but it is not always so clear.

If, prior to or during a counseling meeting, the employee requests to have a representative present, you need to stop and think about the reason you are having the meeting. If you have planned the meeting properly, you will not have to stop to think about it. You will have anticipated the request and developed your response.

If you intend to ask questions of the employee, and they are the types of questions that could lead to disciplinary action, then the meeting is investigative in nature. If you want to continue asking questions, the employee must be allowed to bring in a union representative. You might have no intention of taking a disciplinary action as a result of the meeting. However, your intent doesn't matter. If your questions are investigative in nature, and if the *employee* reasonably believes discipline could result from his answers, you are conducting an investigative meeting as defined in the labor law.

If you are counseling about performance or behavior problems, neither of these should trigger a right to representation.

If the purpose of the meeting is only to counsel, there would be no legal right to a representative. For example, if your objective is to warn an employee about rules violations or to inform the employee of your dissatisfaction with her behavior and your expectations for improvement, you are counseling. If you are meeting to talk about the causes of poor performance and to explore some possible solutions, you are counseling. Neither of these meetings would trigger a right to representation.

In the following example, the supervisor has decided to counsel Chris about his excessive use of sick leave.

> Supervisor: *Chris, you were sick again yesterday, the third Monday in a row. Did you stay home all day?*
>
> Chris: *I want my union representative here before this goes any further.*

Are you counseling or asking an investigative question?

In this simple example, would Chris be entitled to representation? There is no doubt he has such an entitlement. The supervisor has asked a question. If Chris were to admit he felt better at noon and decided to go fishing, he could be subject to a disciplinary action for misuse of sick leave. The supervisor may not have intended to investigate whether his leave use was legitimate. She may simply want to communicate with him about the leave pattern, and the fact that he must improve. However, she asked a question that is investigative in nature, no matter what her intent. If she wants that question, or other questions answered, she will have to give Chris time to contact his representative. On the other hand, if she merely wants to talk with him about the excessive leave, and not investigate whether he is really sick, she can withdraw the question and go on with her counseling without affording him a representative.

In our later chapter on developing a counseling plan, we will explore the need for a counseling objective. A properly stated objective will assist the supervisor in determining the type of meeting she wants to conduct, and whether she will be seeking specific facts from the employee, or merely communicating about a problem and how it might be corrected.

There is much misunderstanding in the workforce about the right to a representative. A large number of employees think they have such a right every time they talk to their supervisors. This simply is not true.

If your employee is covered by a union contract, read it.

If your purpose is to counsel an employee about his behavior or performance, and you want to keep it one on one, you have every right to do so. However, before giving a final answer to the employee's request, do two things. If your employee is covered by a union contract, read it. Some union contracts provide benefits and protections for employees above those provided in law. While the employee might not have a *legal* right to a representative, she could have a *contractual* right. Some contracts even require the supervisor to advise the employee of his right to representation in advance of the meeting. This is rare, but you should check. Second, talk with your human resources advisor, just to be sure. Some organizations have a practice of providing representation for employees almost any time they ask. This may not be wise, but if it's what the organization does, you should follow the practice. Hopefully, you will consult your contract and your advisor prior to the counseling meeting, so that you will be prepared to respond correctly to an employee's request. However, if you are not sure, take a break from the meeting and get some answers. A short delay, although somewhat embarrassing, is better than a wrong answer.

Assuming there is no legal or contractual right to representation, and further assuming there is no policy or practice allowing a representative at a counseling meeting, you now have a practical decision to make. If the employee really believes he needs a representative at the counseling session, and you deny it, what are your chances of having a successful meeting? This will depend on your objective and plan. If all you want to do is inform the employee of a rule or policy, and warn about future violations, it doesn't much matter whether he is cooperative or not. You can get your message across in a directive fashion. However, if your plan calls for a cooperative exchange of ideas about how a performance problem might be resolved, and you deny the requested representation, you might not get the cooperative exchange you wanted.

A representative at a counseling session can be a help or a hindrance.

A representative at a counseling session can be a help or a hindrance. Some see it as their role to interfere. They become argumentative and disruptive. If this happens, and if the employee has no legal right to the representative, you have the right to exclude the representative from the meeting. If the representative is there because the employee enjoys a legal right to have him, your ability to exclude him for improper behavior is limited.

Fortunately, most representatives are reasonable people, and can actually help you accomplish your counseling goals. If the employee truly has a performance or behavior problem, the representative probably is aware of it already. Although she will probably not say so in your presence, she likely will advise the employee to clean up his act. Some people follow the advice of their representatives more readily than that of their superiors. So, on certain occasions, with certain employees, you might see some benefit to allowing a representative to be present at a counseling meeting.

Counseling should be a one on one problem solving effort, at least in its early stages.

Ideally, counseling should be a one on one problem solving effort, at least in its early stages. If you can keep it that way, all the better. When you receive a request for representation at counseling, don't feel that you have to respond immediately. Take some time to think about the kind of meeting you want to hold. Call your human resources advisor, and ask about the legal rights of the employee and the organization's policy. Keep in mind, if you allow representation, even though the employee does not have such a right, you may be starting a practice that the organization does not want. As part of the planning process, think about how you will respond if the employee shows up at the meeting with a representative in tow, without having made a request in advance. Don't hesitate to delay the meeting if you are not sure what to do. Don't let any representative or employee push you to make a hasty decision.

The Aftermath

Don't avoid contact with an employee. It just shows a continuing presence of fear.

Counseling is not a pleasant experience for supervisors. Employees usually don't enjoy it either. One concern often expressed by supervisors is how to interact with the employee after counseling. If she is counseled about attendance problems, she is probably not going to leave the session in a happy frame of mind. If he is warned about the future consequences of his abusive language, it will take some time to get over it. What should the supervisor do in the few hours or days following a counseling meeting?

The biggest mistake you can make at this point is to avoid contact with the employee. Avoidance only shows the continuing presence of fear. There are two things you want to do immediately after conducting a counseling meeting. First, without being too obvious about it, observe the employee's behavior or performance in regard to the matter which brought about the counseling. For example, if you counseled him about long lunches, keep an eye on the extent of his lunch periods for a few days. Look to see whether you are getting at least a short term improvement, or whether you are meeting with outward defiance. Most employees do make a short term adjustment right after counseling. However, a few want to give you an immediate message that they have no intention of changing. If this is what you see, your response must be very quick and decisive. Open defiance must be met with disciplinary action.

The second thing you must do is more difficult. Maintain a business as usual approach. While you are observing the employee's response to the counseling, all other aspects of your relationship must be normal. Don't avoid giving work assignments in your usual manner. Don't stop hanging around the coffee pot every morning, if that is what you usually do. The message you want to convey is that the problem has been addressed, but in working on that problem no other aspects of your relationship with that employee have changed.

Open defiance from an employee after a counseling session must be met with disciplinary action.

CHAPTER SUMMARY

✓ Experiencing a certain amount of fear before counseling is quite natural. Harness your fear through careful planning for the counseling meeting.

✓ Be prepared with facts to prove there is a performance or conduct problem. Many employees refuse to acknowledge the problem until they see the proof.

✓ Make sure you set aside enough time for the meeting. Generally, performance counseling takes more time than counseling about a conduct issue.

✓ Find an adequate private space for your meeting, but don't worry that other employees might know you are counseling a coworker.

✓ Think about how you will respond if the employee requests representation. Most counseling meetings do not trigger a right to representation.

✓ Keep a careful eye on the employee's behavior after the counseling. Be prepared to follow up if you don't see improvement.

THE NECESSITIES

Chapter 2

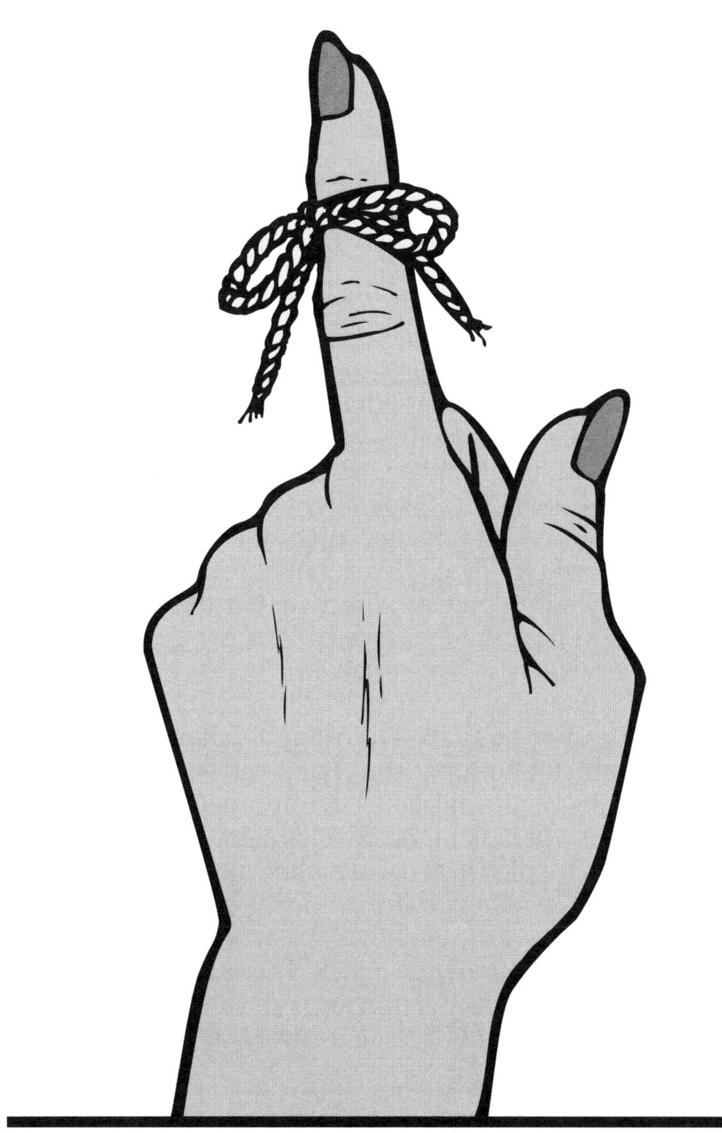

Again, the points made in this chapter will apply whether you are engaged in counseling to improve a person's conduct or performance. Later, when you read the chapters focusing on specific problems and counseling methods, be sure to review this chapter.

Shut Up and Listen

The more you say, the more you will have to defend.

This point could be made more delicately, perhaps. However, the single biggest weakness of supervisors in counseling, grievance meetings, meetings with EEO counselors, and almost every other type of confrontation, is they talk too much. Here is one rule you should always keep in mind when engaged in confrontation. *The more you say, the more you will have to defend.* You might think that, because you are the initiator of most counseling meetings, the burden is upon you to keep the conversation going. This is not always the case. There are times you will want to be very directive, but there are many times you will want to hear the employee's story, or get the employee's view of how a problem might be solved.

It is relatively easy to be a talker. Most of us have little difficulty defining a problem, stating supporting facts, and suggesting a solution. But this is not always the most effective approach to counseling. In a later chapter, we will look at the development of a counseling plan. One aspect of such a plan is to decide who will do most of the talking in the counseling meeting. There are many times it should not be you. If the plan calls for the employee to carry the ball, you are going to have to resist the natural urge to talk. This is much easier said than done, but it is a skill you must cultivate if you are to be effective when counseling employees, or engaging in any kind of employment confrontation.

Many times, you will want to hear the employee's story or view of how a problem might be solved.

There are many books on the market on how to listen effectively, far too many to summarize or even list. You really should read one or two of them. Most people consider themselves good listeners. In reality, they are much better talkers. This is particularly true of supervisors when they engage in employee counseling. You've spent a lot of time observing the employee's conduct or performance.

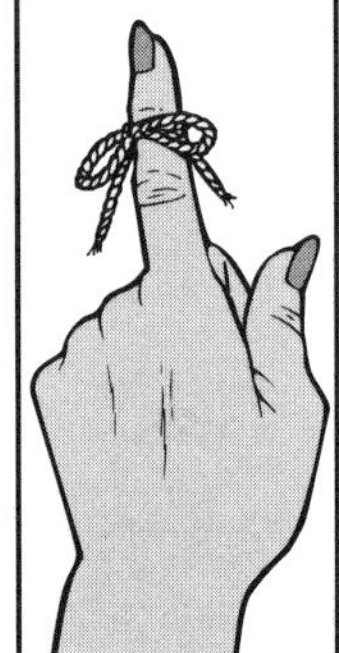

Effective listening calls for behaviors that are unnatural for many of us.

You've worried about it, and thought about how the problem might be solved. Last night, you lost sleep thinking about the upcoming counseling meeting. Now, it is only natural that in the counseling meeting, you will carry the ball. You're all prepared to do so.

When your plan calls for the directive approach to counseling, you probably will do most of the talking. However, when the non-directive approach is more appropriate, you will need all the listening skills you can acquire. Effective listening calls for behaviors that are unnatural for many of us. In a later chapter, we will look at some of the techniques you can employ to make yourself a more effective non-directive counselor, when it is appropriate.

If you are not yet familiar with the terms directive and non-directive, as they pertain to counseling styles, don't let our use of them confuse you at this point. Both approaches will be explored thoroughly in upcoming chapters.

Appear To Be Listening

You certainly have encountered some people who may hear everything you say, but have all the appearances of not listening. Some people can read a document and carry on a conversation on an unrelated subject at the same time. Others can stare out the window and hear every word you say. These people may be good listeners, but they sure don't look interested. What are the chances they are going to get the full story if they don't appear interested? Are they going to hear a condensed version, with many facts omitted, so the speaker can get out of the room quickly?

A theorist once suggested that 75 percent of all communication between individuals is non-verbal. In the 1970s, one of the most popular books on the market was entitled *Body Language,* and there have been numerous others written on the subject in the intervening years. Maybe this aspect of listening has been overdone, but it is a factor you must consider if you are to be successful at employee confronta-

Show you are interested in what the employee is saying.
Take notes.
Nod or grunt.
Have no interruptions.

tions. If you are going to get full, honest input from an employee, you must have the appearance of being interested.

In a business setting, note taking is an effective way of showing interest. Even if the employee is not saying anything noteworthy, just jotting down a few points tends to keep him talking. On the other hand, those supervisors who feel the need to write down almost every word said in a counseling meeting have the opposite impact. If you are so busy writing, you can't possibly be listening. Note taking is an important counseling skill, but it is not a simple one. You have to practice. It can be very useful to keep the conversation going. However, if used inappropriately, it can be a barrier.

Some employees find note taking by the supervisor threatening. Instead of encouraging them to keep talking, it causes them to be more careful. When taking notes, try to observe their effect on the employee. If she is becoming more cautious, put the notes away and summarize the discussion privately after it has concluded.

Nods and grunts, if not overused, can indicate interest and keep the employee talking. Public speakers will tell you they search out people in the audience who nod during the presentation. Here, we are not talking about people who are nodding off to sleep. Rather, speakers focus on listeners who nod their head in agreement, or at least understanding. The same principle applies in counseling. An occasional nodding of the head, or use of responses such as *"uh-huh, yes, I see"* indicate interest in what is being said. You must be careful to convey interest, not necessarily agreement, when using these techniques.

Finally, you must be sure that counseling sessions have no interruptions. There is nothing that indicates a lack of full interest more than a phone call right in the middle of the session, or someone popping into the room to remind you of another meeting.

Effective counseling requires uninterrupted attention to the problem and its resolution.

Many supervisors make the mistake of trying to soften the blow by using vague language.

Use Clear Language

When they finally bring themselves to counsel a misbehaving or poorly performing employee, many supervisors want to soften the blow by couching their criticisms in vague language.

> *"Overall, you're doing a good job, we just need to work a little on your writing skills."*

What message is being given to the employee by this statement? First, the employee is hearing that he is doing a good job, but apparently has one small problem. Is this the message the supervisor intends to convey? Also, note the use of the word *we.* Does the supervisor really intend to say a joint effort will be made to improve the employee's writing, or is this just an attempt to make the criticism sound less harsh? Finally, does the employee know specifically what is wrong with his writing?

> *"George, I have had to return three of your recent reports because the conclusions were very unclear. You are going to have to improve your writing."*

Make sure the employee knows where the real weakness is, and the real purpose of the counsel-ing.

This is a much better beginning to a meeting convened to discuss the employee's performance in this element of his job. First of all, it doesn't attempt to minimize the problem by mixing it with other aspects of his performance. If he is having problems with his writing, the fact that he is performing other components of his job acceptably is not relevant at this point. The statement of the problem is more concrete. *The employee's written conclusions don't make sense.* Now he knows what the rest of the discussion is going to be about, and what he must improve. Although this statement sounds harsher than the first one, it should be more helpful to the employee in the long run. He knows where the real weakness is, and the real purpose of the counseling. The first statement does nothing but confuse the issue. Certainly, the supervisor will be working with him to help improve his writing, but the careful use of the word *you* indicates to the employee where the ultimate responsibility lies.

Clear, direct language is more useful to both parties in the counseling process.

"Mary, you have all the talent in the world; you just aren't getting enough times at bat to get the hits you need."

This is a popular counseling tactic. Here, the supervisor is obscuring his criticism by using sports terminology. What is Mary to learn from this observation? Is she being told she doesn't work hard enough? Perhaps she is not contacting the right people. Maybe the supervisor is saying it's all his fault for not assigning her enough work. Mary would have a much greater chance of improving her performance if she were to hear the criticism more directly.

"Mary, you know the product well enough, but you don't make the number of contacts necessary to make the sales I expect of you."

Clear, direct language is more useful to both parties. First, it helps keep the counseling meetings shorter. It defines the problem and minimizes unnecessary game playing. It allows the employee to focus her improvement efforts. It is more difficult for the employee to claim later that she didn't understand the supervisor's expectations. When you find the need to criticize someone, you will have that normal human tendency to be obscure. You will want to state the problem in such a way that it doesn't hurt as much. However, you must recognize that this approach does neither party a service.

Clear language defines the problem and allows the employee to focus her improvement efforts.

Be Careful With Praise

If you were summoned to your boss' office tomorrow, and the meeting began with the boss saying, *"I want you to know what a good job I think you're doing as unit supervisor,"* what would be your first thought? Upon hearing this type of opening, most people listen for the inevitable*" ...but there is one small problem we must discuss."*

What is the boss trying to do with this approach? Without a doubt, she is following the guidance contained in almost every book and article ever written about employee counseling. You are supposed to

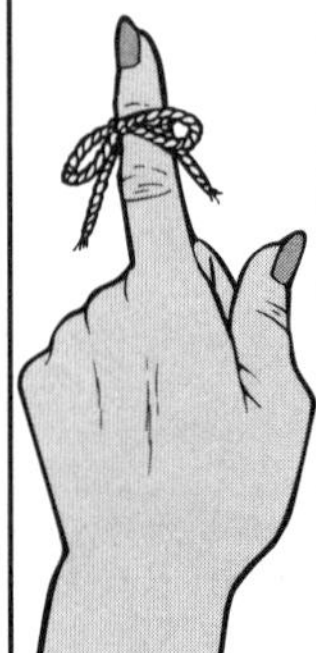

make people feel good about themselves overall. The way to do this is to mix praise with your counseling. Some experts tell you to begin with praise; others tell you to praise the employee at the end of the session, to let him feel good when he leaves. A few suggest making a sandwich of the process using praise at the opening, criticism in the middle, and praise at the end. Most of this is nonsense.

Most people recognize praise at the beginning of a counseling meeting as a set up. And they resent it.

First, most people recognize praise at the beginning of a counseling meeting as a set up. People resent being treated as stupid. Supervisors who lead off with praise are being phony, and everyone knows it. Obviously, the intent behind early praise is to soften the blow. It doesn't work. It's the oldest, most obvious trick in the book. Even if the praise is true and sincerely intended, it is viewed as phony. Sometimes, supervisors try so hard to find something to praise, they actually lie to the employee. Some people don't deserve any praise. It doesn't do anyone any good to invent false praise.

When you counsel, you are doing so because there is a problem. Attack the problem; don't hide it. Praise, while designed to make people feel good about themselves, can actually mislead them into thinking they are doing better than they are. If not handled properly, praise can make a big problem seem minimal. While praise may make people feel better in the short term, the objective of counseling is to solve a problem. Anything that gets in the way of the objective damages the employee in the end.

If not handled properly, praise can make a big problem seem minimal.

That having been said, you should recognize that praise can and should be used under certain conditions. First, it must be sincere. If the employee is doing poorly in his writing, but does very well in face to face dealings with clients, that might be pointed out at some point during the counseling. Second, praise must *look* sincere. As mentioned earlier, the old game of leading with praise looks phony. Praise must be used in a counseling meeting at a time when it appears to be honest. Usually, you will find an opportunity toward the end of a session to compliment the employee for her contributions. But remember to do so only if you are telling the truth.

Remember, use praise only if you are telling the truth. It must be sincere.

Recognize there will be times when praise is completely unwarranted, even if true. If an employee commits a serious violation of policy, using abusive language toward a customer, for example, you want to attack the violation clearly and directly. Beginning, or even ending, with a recounting of the employee's strengths weakens your message.

Whether or not to praise should be part of the planning process. What would you hope to achieve through praise? At what point will you do it? How will you tie it in with the specific problem that is causing the counseling? How can you do it and make it appear sincere? People are not fools. Sure, they want to be told how they contribute positively to the organization. However, they don't want you to play phony games with them.

Know Your Limitations

Most supervisors are not psychologists, although you almost have to be to get by in supervision these days. Your job is to use the counseling process to help an employee correct deficiencies in his performance or conduct. Counseling is an effective tool, to which the majority of employees respond positively. However, some problems experienced by employees at work have their origins elsewhere. Attendance sometimes goes bad because of marital or other family problems. Failure to perform up to expectations can be caused by the abuse of alcohol or drugs.

Restrict your counseling efforts to identified performance or behavioral problems related to the employee's work.

Most supervisors are not prepared to counsel employees on these problems. Restrict your counseling efforts to identified performance or behavioral problems related to the employee's work. If, in the course of your counseling efforts, it becomes apparent the employee has other problems not related to work that may be impacting his work situation, you must encourage him to get help from qualified professionals.

Encourage an employee to seek help elsewhere for personal problems.

For example, if you are counseling an employee about declining performance, and he identifies recent marital difficulties as a possible contributing factor, you would be making a serious mistake to delve into it. This should be treated by people who are trained in a different kind of counseling. Most supervisors would be doing a tremendous disservice to the employee if they were to try to provide advice in this area. Your job is to concentrate on his performance and conduct, and to encourage him to seek help elsewhere to deal with other problems. Almost every government agency has an Employee Assistance Program available to deal with personal problems.

In a later chapter, we will look briefly at some additional steps you should take if you suspect problems at work are caused by alcohol or drug abuse. For now, the important thing to remember is that you are qualified to counsel employees on their work, not on their personal lives.

Document, Document, Document

Counseling will not always bring about the desired change. Most employees respond well to counseling, although some take time before a lasting change happens. Some employees may never attain the skills and abilities necessary to do their jobs. Others will never change their attitudes, and will continue to be attendance problems, disruptive and uncooperative. While these will be the exceptions, you must be prepared to deal with them.

You must be prepared to deal with those employees who will not repsond to counseling.

If counseling doesn't work, a disciplinary or performance based action must follow. This is not to suggest that after one counseling meeting, you will move immediately to discipline if the problem recurs. It is a judgment call how many times to counsel a person before beginning a formal action. Counseling is a process, and change may not come immediately. Some violations by an employee are serious enough to warrant disciplinary action on a first or second occurrence. Others leave room for tolerance and patience.

Make it a practice to document every counseling session you hold with an employee.

Whatever the seriousness of the problem, you should make it a practice to document every counseling session you hold with an employee. This is for your own protection. Counseling is difficult. It is even more difficult to take the next step and initiate formal action when counseling fails. Having done all this work, you don't want to lose a grievance or appeal because you can't prove you counseled the employee. You should never assume the problem has been solved merely because you counseled the employee. Be prepared to move to the next step, and that next step might be impossible without adequate documentation of your initial efforts to correct the problem.

You don't have to write a book to properly document a counseling meeting.

> *June 3, 1996: Bill Fleming took a long lunch—12 PM to 2:30 PM—I talked with him about it—he claimed his watch stopped and he lost track of time—he apologized and promised it would not happen again—I reminded him of the proper lunch hour and the need to request leave in advance, if he planned to be gone longer. He asked my approval to sign for annual leave. I approved, but told him if the incident were repeated, he would be subject to AWOL charges.*

> *July 3, 1996: got complaints from two supervisors, Hanek and Skraps, about K. McDaniel's abrupt behavior in dealing with them on the Smith case. When I discussed it with her, she agreed that she was somewhat discourteous, but blamed it on the customers' impatience with her advising them to proceed more slowly. I reminded her that it was her responsibility to maintain her composure when dealing with impatient clients, and that learning to deal effectively with such people was a key element of her job. She said she agreed and promised to do better. Because this was a first complaint of this nature, I will take no further action at this time.*

Never assume the problem has been solved just because you counsel an employee.

Documenting a session will show the employee is aware of the policy and of the supervisor's expectations.

These brief notes are sufficient documentation of counseling sessions for minor rules violations. They contain everything necessary to prove the employee was properly counseled, including the date of the violation, a brief statement of the facts, the supervisor's actions and the employee's response. Of course, if the violation is repeated, and more counseling is done, the documentation might get more detailed, but you should address the same four factors in any subsequent documentation. Documenting performance discussions may need to be more elaborate. The point is: You don't have to make a transcript of a counseling meeting to prove it has been done.

Such notes take only a few minutes to make. In the example above, if Bill continues his long lunches or other attendance violations, his supervisor evokes disciplinary action, and Bill files a grievance, the supervisor is in an excellent position to prove he counseled Bill about the violation. This will show that he was aware of the policy, and that he also was aware of the supervisor's expectations. That is all the supervisor will need to win a grievance.

Supervisors frequently worry about the legality of these notes. Must the employee be given a copy for it to be used later? The answer to that question is, generally, "no." The note is for the supervisor to use to refresh her memory if the violation is repeated. When it is used to support a formal disciplinary action, the details in the note are subject to challenge by the employee. There is no requirement the employee see the note, or even be aware of it until formal action is taken. An exception might be found in your union contract, if you supervise employees represented by a union. Some contracts require that employees be given copies of supervisors' notes soon after they are created. This does not make your documentation any more difficult. In fact, it actually makes it harder for the employee to challenge the facts if he is given the note soon after the counseling meeting. Read your union contract and check with your labor relations advisor to be sure about your obligations!

There is no requirement that an employee see a supervisor's notes.

Don't make an official file of your notes.

Doesn't the Privacy Act prevent federal government supervisors from keeping documentation that has not been shown to the employee? Again, the answer is no. Federal courts have upheld supervisors' rights to keep memory jogging notes about employee conduct and performance, even without the employee's immediate awareness of the existence of the notes. To comply with the Privacy Act, you should avoid creating a new system of records containing these notes. Don't make an official file for them. Keep all your notes about employees in one common location. Don't create a file for each employee. Each employee's name is on the note, but not on the file. That way, you have not developed a system of records which might have to be declared under the Privacy Act.

One innovative manager kept what he called his *shoebox notes.* When he found it necessary to counsel an employee, he made a short note to document the counseling. Then he took the note home and put it in a shoebox under his bed. If he had to resort to disciplinary action against an employee who did not respond to the counseling, he searched through his shoebox retrieving the notes having to do with the counseling of that employee. The notes were then used to create a formal disciplinary action such as a reprimand. The information was transferred to the reprimand. The notes could then be destroyed, or placed into an official discipline file, to which the employee then would have full access. That manager was able to keep the records he needed, and, at the same time, honor the employee's rights under the Privacy Act.

Short notes for your own use and possbile future reference are all you need.

Some supervisors have a practice of writing a confirming letter to an employee after a counseling meeting. In most cases, this is too much work. When you find a need to counsel an employee several times for similar offenses, and you begin to envision disciplinary action as the only alternative, letters confirming counseling meetings might be appropriate. But, in the early stages, when you are merely trying to resolve a small problem, you don't need this formal, extensive documentation. Short notes for your own use and possible future reference are all you need.

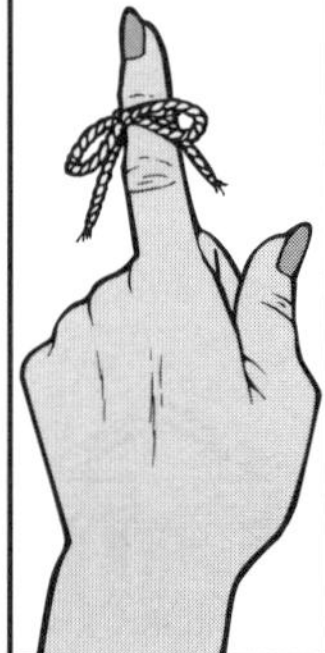

In the state and local arena, there will be similar situations, but they will vary according to state law and the collective bargaining agreement.

CHAPTER SUMMARY

✓ Decide in advance whether you should do most of the talking or whether you will require the employee to take the lead. This will depend upon whether you are counseling to correct a performance problem or a conduct problem.

✓ Your body language and mannerisms have an impact on whether you will meet your counseling objective. Not only must you listen carefully; you must have the appearance of listening.

✓ Use direct language to describe a problem. Vague language used to soften the blow does neither party a service.

✓ Use praise carefully. Employees often view praise as a phony attempt to set them up for the bad news to follow. If used, praise must be sincere and well timed.

✓ Avoid getting involved in an employee's personal problems that may be affecting his performance or conduct at work. Focus on the problems at work, and refer the employee to other sources to deal with personal problems.

✓ Document every counseling meeting. Note the date of the meeting, the problem you discussed, the employee's response and any commitments made. Documentation does not have to be elaborate. However, if there is no improvement, more detailed documentation will be necessary as the counseling process continues.

✓ Keep your counseling notes in an unmarked file. Avoid the creation of a system of records that could violate the Privacy Act.

DIRECTIVE AND NON-DIRECTIVE METHODS AND WHEN TO USE THEM

Chapter 3

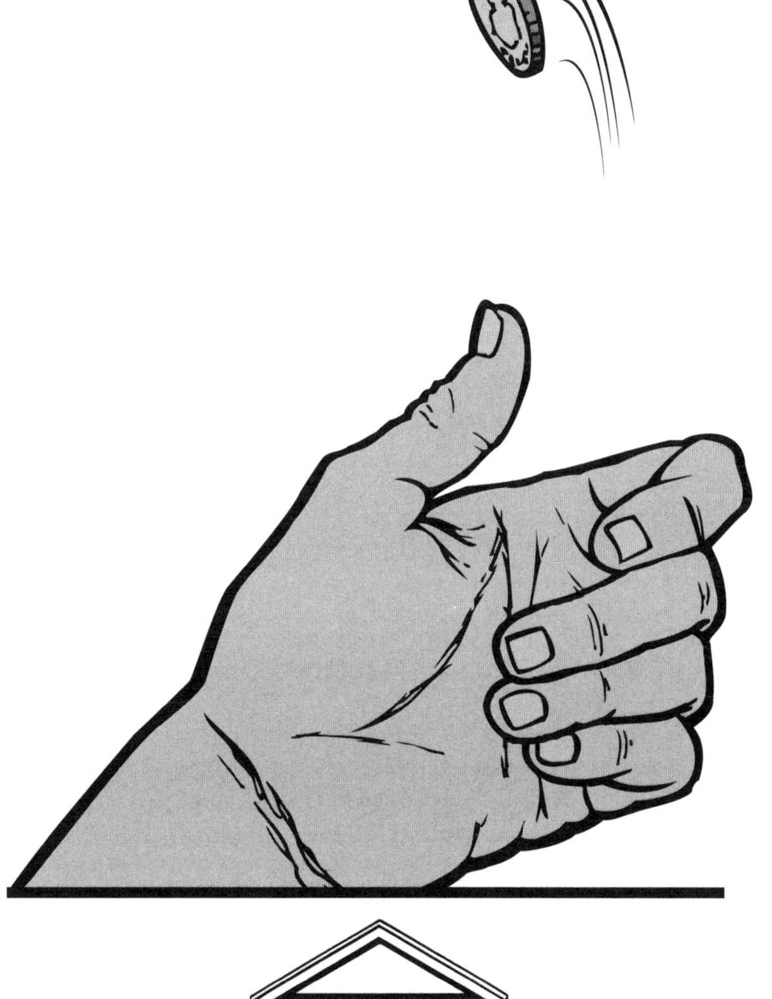

The supervisors who are most successful at employee counseling use the style and approach that best fits the situation.

Some supervisors believe their own personality should be the driving force behind the counseling approach that will be used. For example, if you are generally very direct with people, that is the most appropriate counseling style for you. If you are a natural listener, then that's the approach to use. *This is the wrong way to view counseling.* The supervisors who are most successful at employee counseling are those who are able to use the style and approach that best fits the situation. The situation is determined by the type of problem you are confronting and the employee causing the problem. Failing to adapt your style to the situation will often put you on the wrong path from the very start of the process.

The terms *directive counseling* and *non-directive counseling* have been used several times already. In this chapter, we will give them meaning, outline their differences, and explain when each is most appropriate.

DIRECTIVE COUNSELING

The supervisor controls the direction and content of the meeting.

Professional counselors would view this as too simplistic, but in its most basic terms, the directive approach to counseling can be summed up as: *"I talk, you listen."*

When the directive method is used, the supervisor will lead the counseling session, usually doing most of the talking. The supervisor will tell the employee what the rules are, describe the employee's behavior that necessitated the counseling meeting, and advise the employee of the behavior the supervisor expects in the future. The employee will not necessarily sit silently. He will be allowed to ask questions, give his side of the story and, of course, argue his case if he believes the supervisor is wrong. However, the bottom line is that the supervisor controls the direction and content of the meeting.

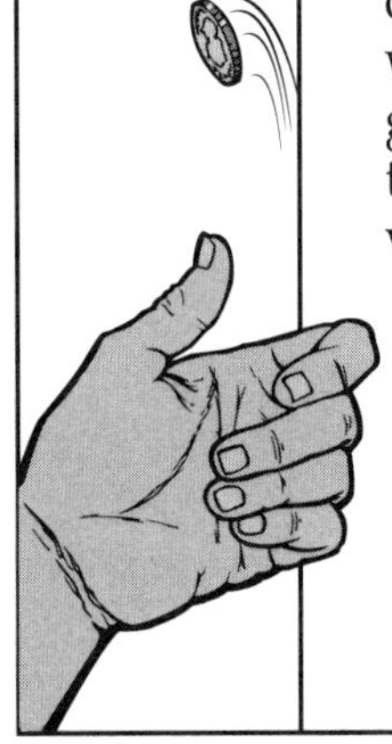

Even though the supervisor is in the driver's seat in directive counseling, it does not stifle employee input.

Directive counseling meetings are usually brief. They are usually well planned. The supervisor knows in advance what he is going to say, although he has to be prepared for a variety of employee responses.

Generally speaking, the directive counseling method is appropriate when you are counseling an employee about a conduct problem. Attendance problems, discourtesy, disruptive behavior and similar problems are usually best handled through the directive method. The supervisor can readily identify the behavior causing the problem, and is prepared to list specific examples. The supervisor is able to describe how that behavior affects the work of the unit. Finally, the supervisor is prepared to tell the employee the type of behavior that will be considered acceptable in the future, as well as the consequences of not conforming to the supervisor's wishes. There really isn't much for the employee to say.

The directive approach does not stifle employee input. The employee is free to challenge the supervisor's facts or the reasonableness of the policy. The employee is free to get clarifications about what is expected. Certainly, the employee is free to argue the fairness of the policy as it is applied to him, in comparison to others. However, as you can see, using the directive approach, the supervisor is in the driver's seat.

Non-directive counseling turns some of the leadership of the meeting over to the employee.

NON-DIRECTIVE COUNSELING

"You talk; I listen," is the basic way to describe the non-directive method of employee counseling. Using this approach, the supervisor turns some of the leadership of the meeting over to the employee. While the supervisor remains in control of the counseling objective, responsibility is placed on the employee's shoulders to come up with solutions to the problem.

Non-directive counseling is more difficult for supervisors to use successfully.

This method of counseling is more difficult to use successfully. It requires behaviors that are considerably different from directive counseling. Most people find it easier to talk than to listen. *If you are going to use the non-directive method properly, you will have to overcome the urge to talk, and make maximum use of your listening skills.* Don't think you are giving up your supervisory responsibilities when you use the non-directive method. You remain in control of the process, but you share with the employee the responsibility for figuring out how to resolve the problem.

The non-directive approach still requires you to carefully plan the meeting. In fact, it may require more careful planning than the directive method. It definitely requires counseling skills that are difficult to learn, and even unnatural for most people. It requires you to avoid giving solutions to the problem, even if you know what those solutions are. It takes more time and more patience than the directive method.

After this comparison, you are probably wondering why anyone would use the non-directive method, if it is so difficult. The reason is simple. There will be times when you don't want to be responsible for defining the problem and suggesting solutions. Sometimes, it is much more appropriate to place that burden squarely on the employee's shoulders. The theory behind this approach is that, if you expect a lasting solution to a problem, and a solution to which the employee is fully committed, the solution must come from within the employee, and not be dictated by an outside authority.

Though it takes more time and patience, the non-directive approach is the only way to go when dealing with performance difficulties.

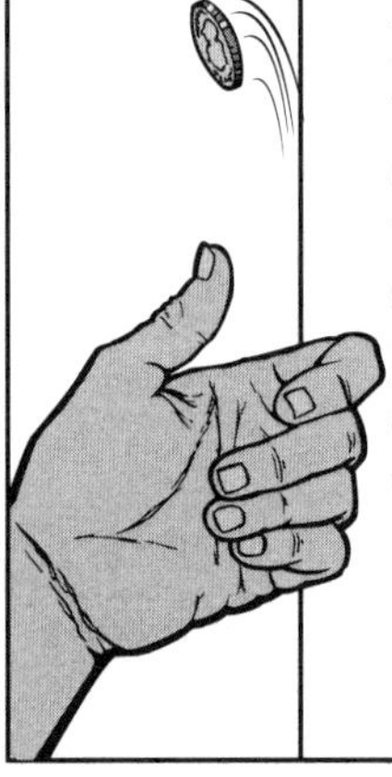

While the directive method is great for handling most conduct problems, the non-directive approach is the only way to go when dealing with performance difficulties. You can use the directive method to communicate rules and expectations. You can get compliance from the employee by stating the consequences of future violations. However, if you truly are looking for someone to improve her performance, you must require her to look inside and figure out for herself why she is not performing, and you must allow her to figure out what to do about it.

Non-directive counseling is coaching... helping the employee see the problem, figure out its causes and plan solutions.

Earlier, we suggested that the most crucial decision you make before you begin the counseling process is whether you are dealing with someone who doesn't care or someone who wants to, but can't quite do things right. People who don't care, people with attitude problems, people who ignore the rules of the organization, are candidates for the directive approach. However, employees who really want to do a good job, but lack some knowledge or skill, must be given the opportunity to solve their own problem. In a nutshell, you can direct people to follow the rules, but you cannot direct them to improve their performance if they don't have the capabilities.

You are familiar with the term *coaching.* Some years ago, it became a fad management word. Well, used properly, coaching is not a fad. It's what the non-directive counseling method is all about. Helping the employee to see a problem, figure out its causes and plan solutions is coaching. Telling someone what to do to resolve a problem is dictating. Unfortunately, most supervisors are more natural dictators than coaches.

When you use the non-directive method, you will employ some techniques that may not be necessary for directive counseling. Although both approaches require you to listen, you must be a much better listener to be successful at non-directive counseling. You also will need to use techniques to keep the employee talking. Paraphrasing, probing and silence are some of these. In our chapter on performance counseling, we will explore these, and other techniques in greater depth.

CHAPTER SUMMARY

✓ If you are truly attempting to resolve a problem, you must use the approach that is best suited to the situation, not the one with which you are more comfortable.

✓ Behavioral problems usually are best tackled using the directive approach. Performance problems generally call for the non-directive approach.

✓ Prior to the counseling meeting, you must consciously choose which method is most appropriate. However, you should avoid going to the extreme with either method.

✓ The characteristics of the individual employee also will influence your choice of approach. Some people like to talk; others need encouragement.

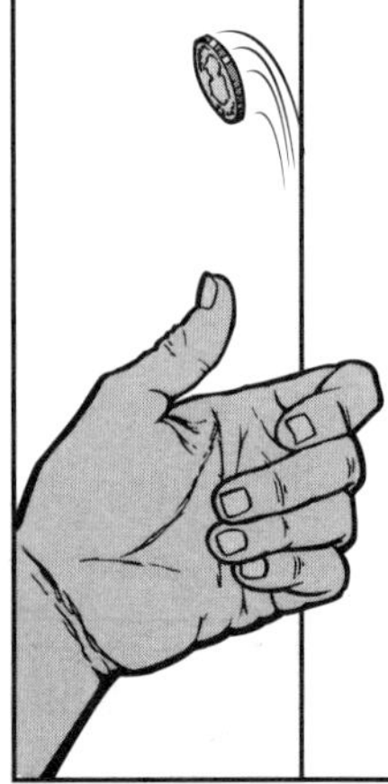

THE COUNSELING PLAN

Chapter 4

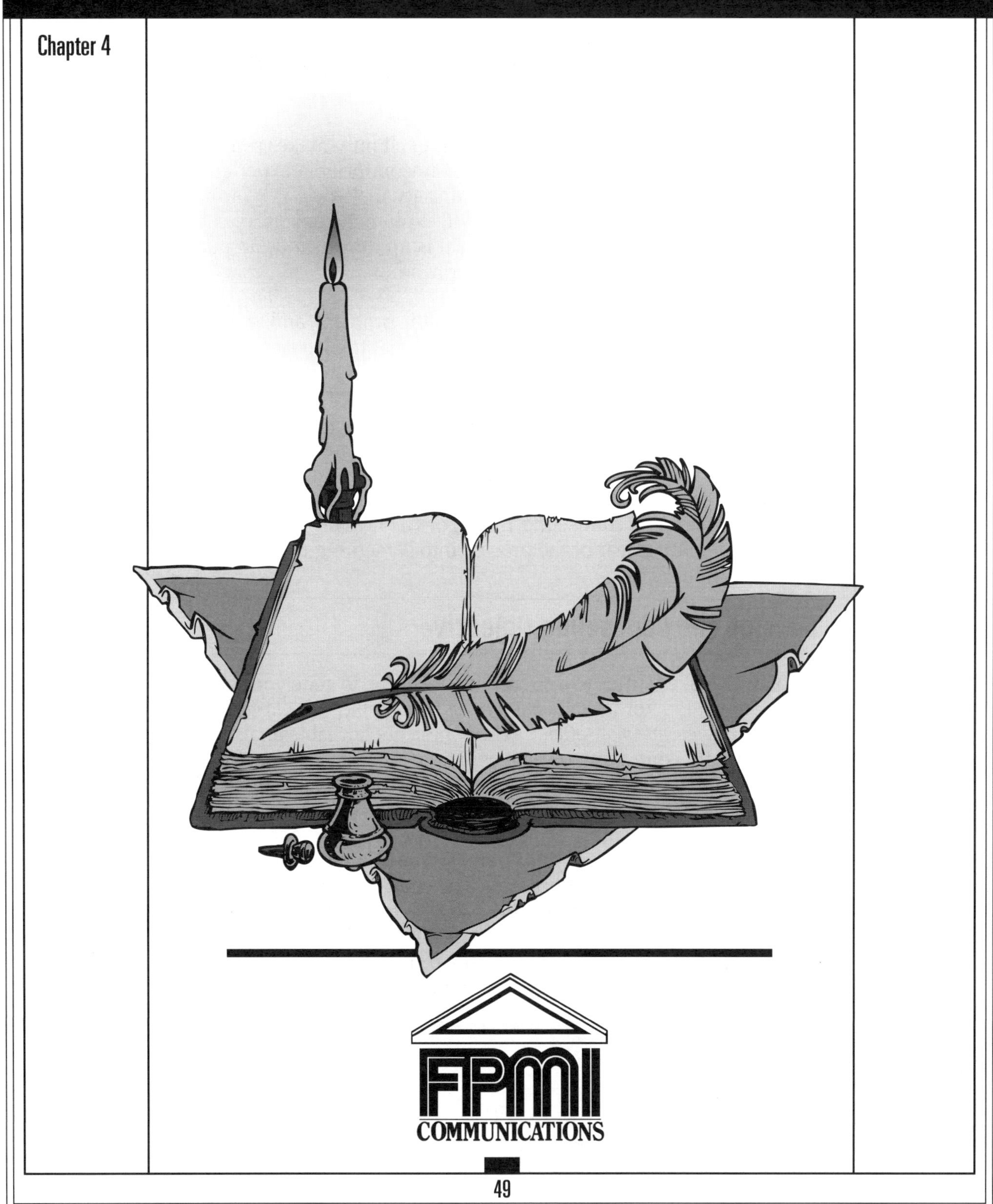

Lack of planning almost guarantees you will be on the defensive after the meeting begins.

Supervisors draw up plans for many things. It only makes sense, as you begin one of the most difficult and uncomfortable experiences you will ever face in your supervisory capacity, that you will be armed with some sort of plan. This chapter will explore the necessary components of a counseling plan. The format is up to you. You can put it in writing, or merely map it out in your head.

Sometimes supervisors get so involved in the problem, and worry so much about the counseling meeting, they forget to plan properly for the confrontation. In their rush to get it over with, they lose sight of why they are doing it. Lack of planning almost guarantees that you will be on the defensive once the meeting begins. Some employees are real experts at putting you on the defensive. Some are so good at it, the meeting ends with the supervisor apologizing for having put the employee through the counseling experience. Planning doesn't guarantee successful counseling, but it goes a long way toward channeling your natural fear of the process into something useful.

Develop the Counseling Objective

Focus on what you want to achieve in the specific counseling session.

If you were asked, prior to a counseling meeting, to state your objective, you would likely say *"to improve his performance"* or *"to get her to come to work on time more often."* While these are laudable goals, they are not proper counseling objectives. These are your reasons for engaging in the counseling process. They will do nothing to help you in the counseling meeting you are about to enter. What you need to focus on is what you want to achieve in the specific counseling session that lies ahead. We will call this your *meeting objective.* Its purpose is to get you to focus in the short term. The counseling process may or may not result in a resolution of the problem that brings you and the employee together. However, if you have established your meeting objective properly, you can assess your progress on an incremental basis as you go through the counseling process.

In your initial meeting, you should advise the employee there is a problem and what your expectations for improvement are.

Problem A

Dean is absent frequently. If he's not sick, he has a sick child, or a flat tire or some other emergency. You never know until the work day begins whether you can count on his presence. If you were about to counsel Dean on this problem, what would be the most appropriate meeting objective?

Choice 1.

To find out why Dean is so frequently absent.

Choice 2.

To find out if Dean would like to change his work schedule.

Choice 3.

To advise Dean there is a problem, and to let him know your expectations for improvement.

Choice 4.

To let Dean know he could be fired if this continues.

You likely will be inclined to go with Choice 1. This seems like the humane thing to do. Let's see what Dean's problem really is, and whether he needs our help to resolve it. Choice 1 is a wrong answer. Dean's problem is not the issue that necessitated the counseling. Your problem is that Dean is not at work when you need him and expect him. You must let him know this is a problem and that improvement is expected. Choice 3 is the correct objective.

If all of this sounds somewhat uncaring, keep in mind you are developing a personal counseling objective for your initial meeting with the employee. In that meeting, Dean may wish to reveal the real reasons he is not coming to work. If he does so, that is his business. Perhaps he will suggest a schedule change. If so, you have something to think about. However, if you are only going to achieve one thing in the few minutes you will meet with Dean, it must be Choice 3.

You must leave the meeting with your objective accomplished or you have wasted your time.

You must think about yourself first as you enter a counseling meeting. What do you want to get out of it? That is your meeting objective. If other things happen, that's just fine. But you must leave this meeting with that objective accomplished; otherwise you have wasted your time.

Problem B

Vicki is a technically competent employee. However, she drives her coworkers crazy. She is belligerent and uncooperative. The end result is that people stay away from her, even when they should be consulting her. This negatively impacts the success of the office. In counseling Vicki, what would be your meeting objective?

Choice 1.

To let her know how her behavior impacts the work, and the changes you require.

Choice 2.

To determine whether she should be referred to the Employee Assistance Program.

Choice 3.

To find out whether her coworkers are to blame.

Choice 4.

To discuss the possibility of reassignment.

If you picked Choice 1, you've caught on to the intent of a meeting objective. It is possible that choices 2, 3 or 4 could be ultimate resolutions to the problem. But they are not the purpose of this counseling meeting with Vicki. If you will achieve nothing else in the upcoming meeting, you must achieve the objective found in Choice 1.

Performance problems require coaching. Improvement cannot begin by telling the employee what to do.

Problem C

Gary is not meeting minimum performance standards in a critical element of his job. In two other elements, he is barely acceptable. Which of these is the best meeting objective?

Choice 1.

To improve his performance.

Choice 2.

To let him know he's doing poorly, and outline the improvements you expect.

Choice 3.

To have him identify the causes of his poor performance, and outline some steps he will take to improve.

Choice 4.

To discuss the possibility of placing him in another position.

If you chose Choice 1, you've made the mistake of developing a long term objective, not a meeting objective. Go back to the beginning of the chapter and reread.

If you chose Choice 2, you were hooked into a wrong answer because you went along with the pattern set by Problems A and B. Performance problems are different from conduct problems, and require a different approach to counseling. You may want to review the previous chapter.

If you chose Choice 4, you have completely missed the point. You are looking for solutions before you talk about the problem.

The supervisor is a helper, not a dictator in the performance improvement process.

Choice 3 is the one and only way to do it, assuming we believe that Gary really has the desire to do a good job. This is a performance problem. Gary must be coached. Improvement cannot begin by telling him what to do. He must be helped to identify why he is having performance problems. And he must be given the responsibility to find ways to improve. The supervisor is a helper, not a dictator in this process.

We could go on with more examples, but you should get the message by now. Develop an objective for yourself that states what you want to accomplish in the specific counseling meeting you are about to have. If other objectives might be met, that's a bonus. You must walk in with your objective in mind. Before writing your objective, determine whether you are dealing with a conduct or performance problem. If it's performance, remember that long term performance improvement must come from within the employee. Your meeting objective should allow that process to begin.

Determine Whether You Will Use the Directive or Non-Directive Approach

Your approach to the meeting will flow directly from your objective.

Once you have developed a sound meeting objective, this decision is easy. The approach you will use flows directly from your objective. If your objective calls for you to identify problems employees are causing, letting them know about rules, or telling them your expectations for improvement, the directive approach is warranted. This is the approach you should use with Dean and Vicki.

If, on the other hand, your objective is to require the employee to establish his own improvement plan, as in Gary's case, the non-directive approach is appropriate.

Remember, in the preceding chapter we said that the employee also must be considered. Being directive does not mean the employee has nothing to say.

Remember, the approach you decide to use is not rigid, but it will determine how the major part of the meeting will be conducted.

For example, perhaps Vicki likes to talk. You might choose to open the meeting with a question in order to give her the chance to talk. *"Why is there so much friction between you and the others?"* might be a good start. Although this is a non-directive opening, and your objective calls for the directive approach, you will be prepared to switch to the directive method after Vicki has had the chance to tell her story.

The approach you decide to use is not rigid. It does not always dictate how you will begin the counseling session. It does determine how the major part of the counseling meeting will be conducted. In Vicki's case, you may give her ample opportunity to speak, but, by the time the meeting ends, you will achieve your objective, using primarily a directive approach.

In Gary's case, your objective requires you to use the non-directive approach to let him do most of the talking. But Gary could be unwilling to let that happen. You may have to resort to some directive techniques to get him started. However, by the time the meeting ends, you will meet your objective, using non-directive counseling.

Write an Opening Statement That Defines the Problem

If you get off on the wrong foot in a counseling meeting, you will find yourself on the defensive quite quickly. Whether you are using the directive or non-directive approach, it's your ball at the beginning of the meeting. You are the one who decided counseling is necessary. So the responsibility is upon you to get things started down the right path. Things would be different if the employee approached you asking to be counseled. That doesn't happen very often.

It is your responsibility to set the meeting on the right path.

Make an opening statement that signals the purpose of the meeting.

First, forget about small talk. Those books that tell you to put the person at ease by talking about the weather or a sporting event must have been written by people who have never done this before. Employees aren't put at ease by that type of talk. They know they are not there for a pleasant conversation. It's like starting with phony praise, as mentioned in an earlier chapter. People know the game; they resent it, and it doesn't work.

In most cases, you want to make an opening statement that signals the purpose of the meeting. Analyze the following exchange.

> Supervisor: *Dean, I want to talk to you today about your use of leave.*
>
> Dean: *What about it?*
>
> Supervisor: *You have the lowest sick and annual leave balance in the section.*
>
> Dean: *So what?*
>
> Supervisor: *Well, it's not good.*
>
> Dean: *Why not? It's there to use isn't it?*
>
> Supervisor: *Well, yes, it's there to use, but you use too much.*
>
> Dean: *What's too much?*

What you are seeing in this exchange is a supervisor who is on the defensive and is likely to stay that way. She may have developed a good objective for the counseling, and she may have planned the proper approach, but her opening statement did nothing but get her in trouble. Dean is being counseled because he frequently takes unplanned days off. His leave balance, and whether he is using sick or

In defining the wrong problem, you can give the employee total control.

annual leave have nothing to do with it. It was the lack of an opening statement that put the discussion immediately on the wrong track. The supervisor called the meeting because there is a problem. However, in defining the wrong problem, she has given Dean total control. It will be tough to get it back.

Here is an improved version of the same opening.

> Supervisor: *Dean, I asked you to come in today because we need to talk about your attendance.*
>
> Dean: *What about it?*
>
> Supervisor: *During the last month, you have taken six days of unscheduled leave.*
>
> Dean: *So what? I've had problems. That's what leave is for, isn't it?*
>
> Supervisor: *My problem is that you're not here when I need you and expect you, and that causes the section's work not to get done.*

Getting on the right track leads to the accomplishment of the meeting objective.

What a difference! Using just a little planning, the supervisor defined the problem as Dean's attendance and its impact on the unit's work, not on his use of leave and his leave balance. Notice that the supervisor is not on the defensive. It may, at first, seem like a small point, but it is important to get a counseling meeting started on the right track. In the second example, Dean and his supervisor are on the track that leads to the accomplishment of the supervisor's objective. The discussion will be about the number of days off Dean has taken and their impact on production. In the first example, the discussion could go anywhere.

Your plan must reflect how you anticipate the employee to react.

Be prepared for surprises.

Develop Plan B

As we've seen, several things go into a counseling plan. One factor is, of course, the employee. You know your people well enough that you can anticipate how each is likely to react to your opening statement and to the counseling process, in general. Your plan must reflect this anticipated reaction. However, people can be unpredictable. You must anticipate the employee's likely reaction, and prepare for it. On the other hand, you must have a plan to handle surprises.

Take Gary, as an example. He is a cooperative employee, with a good attitude. He really tries hard. However, as we saw earlier, his performance is a problem. He's trying, but he isn't making it. His supervisor has scheduled a counseling meeting, in which she is planning to use the non-directive method to get Gary talking about what might be the causes of his performance problems. Then she plans to have him identify some things he might do to solve the problem.

Using a technique suggested earlier in this book, she tells him in advance about the meeting, and identifies its purpose. You may remember, we called this the principle of *shared worry.* In this case, her purpose is not to put additional pressure on Gary, but to get him thinking about his performance problems, so that he is better prepared for the meeting. The counseling session begins as follows.

> Supervisor: *Gary, yesterday I asked you to think about some of the problems you are having with the work, so that we could discuss some possible solutions today. What have you come up with?*
>
> Gary: *Well, I thought about it a lot last night, and I guess I didn't realize I have performance problems. I don't understand why we're having this meeting.*

Remember, denial is a normal human reaction to criticism.

This isn't what the supervisor anticipated. Gary is usually very cooperative. She expected him to come in and acknowledge there are certain problems, so they could get right down to business. She was trying to get right into non-directive counseling, by allowing him to take the lead. It didn't work. Gary is either unaware of his shortcomings, or pretending to be. What does she do next?

Even in dealing with a cooperative employee, she should have been prepared for this. As mentioned earlier, denial is a normal human reaction to criticism. Even the best people don't enjoy counseling. In Gary's mind, if he pleads ignorance, maybe she will let him off the hook. However, Gary's supervisor has a Plan B. The discussion continues.

> Supervisor: *Well, Gary, there are problems. Let's take your critical element: report writing. I have had to return five of your last six monthly reports, because the data was either incomplete or the conclusions weren't justified. Your standard calls for a minimal number of returned reports. Five out of six is not minimal. In the element, telephone assistance, you failed to respond to customers' questions within the 24 hour time frame three times this month. Although that is within standard, it is just barely so. These are the things we need to talk about. It doesn't look like good performance to me. What do you think?*

If the employee fails to acknowledge a problem, it is your obligation to state it for him.

The supervisor was ready with Plan B. It would have been better if Gary had acknowledged the above examples, but she was prepared to do so, if he were not willing. She called the counseling meeting. The obligation is upon her to state a problem. She was prepared to do so if Gary failed to acknowledge the problem.

Don't throw your original plan away just because of one setback.

Unfortunately, she has had to revert to a more directive approach to get things started. You must be ready to make an adjustment if the employee fails to respond as you expect. That is why you need Plan B.

However, she should not yet abandon her objective or originally planned approach. Gary's failure to cooperate early is no reason to abandon the plan quickly. Notice, in her last sentence, how she attempts to get back to the non-directive method. Later, we will see whether it works.

The key point to remember is to have a plan and a back up plan. But don't throw your original plan away just because of one setback.

CHAPTER SUMMARY

✓ You should develop a plan for each counseling meeting. Without a plan, you are likely to find yourself on the defensive.

✓ A meeting objective should be established first. This states what you intend to accomplish in the counseling session. It should not be a long term objective.

✓ The meeting objective leads directly to a determination of the appropriate counseling method—directive or non-directive.

✓ You must be prepared with a planned opening statement that clearly defines the problem. If you get on the wrong track, you will be on the defensive for the entire meeting.

✓ The best way to open a counseling meeting is with a statement of your specific observations. Avoid vague or general descriptions of the problem.

✓ You should stick to your plan to the extent possible. However, you must have a back-up plan, in case the employee does not respond as you expected.

COUNSELING TO CHANGE BEHAVIOR

Chapter 5

It is your job to identify and attempt to correct the work behavior of an employee.

An employee with a behavior or conduct problem is one who is inclined not to follow the policies of the organization. Perhaps he uses abusive language in dealing with customers and coworkers. Maybe she is frequently argumentative, or refuses to follow the supervisor's directives. Conduct problems cover a wide spectrum, ranging from minor infractions to the outrageous. When dealing with this type of problem, you are confronting an employee who knows or should know what is expected, but simply refuses to conform. It is possible that the employee's failures are not completely intentional. There may be an underlying cause, such as a mental impairment or alcohol abuse. If there is something beyond the employee's control causing the behavioral problem, it may be revealed during counseling, and it might lead to a different counseling approach, or to a referral to a counseling professional. However, it is your job to identify and attempt to correct the work behavior of the employee. The most appropriate method for doing so is the directive method.

The directive method is the most appropriate in counseling work behavior problems.

Many supervisors agree that the most common behavioral problem deals with employee attendance. The government provides its employees with a reasonable amount of sick and annual leave. In recent years, Congress has provided additional entitlements with legislation such as the Family and Medical Leave Act and the Family Friendly Leave Act. Despite this, some people never seem to have enough leave. Others don't like to follow proper leave request procedures and there are always a few people who can't make it to work on time.

Because of the frequency of attendance related problems, we will use this throughout this chapter. In fact, we will continue to deal with Dean, the employee we discussed in the previous chapter. You will recall that Dean is one of those people who uses a lot of unplanned leave. His supervisor decided her meeting objective is to let him know there is a problem, its effects on the work and her expectations for improvement. This objective should cause her to primarily use the directive approach. She also decided on an opening statement. Turn back a few pages to refresh your memory.

The longer you take to respond to an infraction, the more likely your message becomes weak.

In this chapter, we will highlight more of the do's and don'ts of the directive counseling method. Although we will be dealing specifically with Dean and his attendance problem, the points made will apply to any employee or any problem that requires the use of the directive approach to counseling.

Counsel in a Timely Manner

If you are dealing with a one-time infraction by an employee, the counseling should occur as soon as possible after the infraction. You must take the time you need to gather the facts, but excessive delay lessens the impact of the counseling. Assume you overhear a loud, public argument between two employees. If you wait a week or two to conduct a counseling meeting, you are giving a message that such behavior is not a big deal. Fear of the counseling process causes supervisors to put it off. However, the longer you take to respond to the infraction, the weaker your message.

Some behaviors are ongoing. Poor attendance is an example. Certainly, you are not going to counsel an employee the first time he uses sick leave, or the first time his car breaks down. You know when counseling is warranted. You begin to get that uncomfortable feeling about what you are observing. Now, the only question is, how long will you put it off?

In the previous chapter, we observed a supervisor develop a counseling objective and an opening statement for a counseling meeting with Dean. How long will Dean's supervisor watch the pattern of his leave use before she confronts him with it? The longer she waits, the more she can expect this question from Dean. *"If it's that big a deal, why didn't you say something to me earlier?"* Look who is on the defensive again.

There is nothing you can do about the employee giving his own version of the meeting to his friends.

Keep Counseling Private, But Not Necessarily A Secret

We dealt with space requirements earlier. Do the best you can, under the usual constraints, to find the proper setting. You want a place where the two of you can feel free to talk without others overhearing. (See pages 20 and 21 for a quick review.)

Of course, you know that you can't leave a counseling meeting and discuss it with other employees. Legally speaking, they don't have a need to know. You would be violating the employee's privacy rights if you discussed the problem with those who have no official concern with it. However, you can rest assured that the people will know about it. They won't know all the details, but they will know it happened. There is nothing you can do about the employee giving his own version of the meeting to his friends. But at least the others know you're doing your job.

Counsel the Offender, Not the Group

If you want to lose the respect of the people you supervise, make frequent use of the old practice of calling the group together to talk about a problem, when, in fact, there are only one or two offenders in the work group. Employees see this approach as nothing less than cowardly.

> *"I want to remind all of you about the attendance policies in the office. I see more frequent use of emergency leave, and it puts us in a real bind. The director has noticed it also, and has asked me to issue a reminder. So let's see what we can do to bring things back into line."*

Calling the group together to talk about a problem that only relates to a few offenders is seen as cowardly.

This infuriates people for two reasons. First, they know which of their coworkers is the target of your reminder. What they don't understand is why you don't have the nerve to confront the offender, rather than make innocent employees listen to your speech. Second, no one wants to be confronted by a third party, who claims to be speaking for someone else. If the supervisor has a problem with an employee's behavior, the supervisor should state the problem, not blame the meeting on the director.

Both the group counseling and passing the blame to another level of management are common practices. Both are understandable. Again, the fear factor comes into play. It is easier to speak in general terms to the group rather than sit face to face with the individual employee. And it takes some of the pressure off if you can convince people that you would not be bothering them, but for your boss' unreasonable policies. The problem is these practices don't work. Employees can see right through them. Later, if Dean's attendance doesn't improve, and you try to tell him he should have paid attention to the group counseling, he will claim he had no idea you were referring to his attendance. You're back at square one.

Communicating by means other than a personal confrontation implies the matter is not serious enough to deal with it in person.

Unfortunately, technological advances often bring undesirable results. Many managers now use e-mail to counsel employees. E-mail is an efficient way to exchange information but it is no substitute for face to face counseling. Counseling by computer, whether directed to the group or the offending individual, not only indicates that the supervisor fears the process, but also it communicates to employees that the matter is not serious enough to warrant a personal confrontation.

A complete statement of the problem should include its effects on the organization.

Correctly Identify the Problem and State It at the Outset

Just a reminder: Use clear language and plan an opening statement that defines the purpose of the meeting. In Dean's case, the supervisor has decided to open by telling him she wants to discuss his attendance and its effect on the work. She has avoided identifying the problem as his low leave balance. She has also decided not to ask him why he is absent so frequently. Although he might offer more excuses during the counseling, and they might well discuss problems he identifies, it is not on her agenda.

Also, think about whether the supervisor should use praise in the counseling meeting, and if so, when would be the most appropriate time. Assume that Dean is a technically competent employee, whose work is fine, when he shows up. Would the supervisor begin the meeting by pointing this out? If she does, she has already begun to minimize the problem, or at least to make it more obscure. If Dean's performance is to be mentioned at all, it should be later in the discussion, after the problem and her expectations have been identified.

Remember that a complete statement of the problem should include its effects or likely effects on the organization. Pointing out a violation of policy could bring about a response of *"So What."* Be prepared to talk about why the policy exists and how the organization will be affected if employees don't abide by the policy.

The only way to counter an employee's alleged ignorance of the problem is through the presentation of data.

Have the Facts Ready and Use Them Appropriately

You must be prepared for the alleged ignorance strategy. When Dean is told that his frequent absence is causing production problems, he is likely to argue his absences are not that frequent. The only way to counter this, and to prove there is a problem, is through presenting data. The facts must be directly relevant to the problem statement.

> *"During the past month, you have taken five days off, without scheduling leave in advance. On two of those days, you said you were sick; two were because one of your children was sick, and one was because your car needed repair."*

> *"I had to reassign the XYZ report to Mary to complete, and one day we had to pay someone to stay late to get the ABC ledger out on time."*

This is hard data, and the supervisor should be prepared to use it. It relates directly to her definition of the problem. It shows Dean is taking a lot of unplanned leave, and it proves the organization and other employees have paid a price for it. If the supervisor were not prepared, and had not anticipated the ignorance defense, there would be no way to support the need for counseling. The session would be off to a very shaky start.

Be prepared to hear that the employee is being singled out.

Be Prepared for Comparisons

"Why are you picking on me? Other people use the same amount of leave I do. There are others out there who have lower leave balances than me. Mary is off as many days as I am, and I often have to do her work. This just isn't fair."

This is one of the most common defenses you will face. After you have successfully proven there is a problem, be prepared to hear that the employee is being singled out. What is the proper response?

Response 1.

Yes, Mary takes a lot of time off, but I'm talking with her about that.

Response 2.

We're not talking about Mary. We're talking about you and the problems you cause when you're not here.

Response 3.

You have the lowest sick and annual leave balance in the section.

Response 2 is correct. Simple as it may sound, the only effective response to the comparison defense is not to allow it. You are not there to discuss the problems of other employees or your efforts to resolve them. Even if Response 1 is the truth, it isn't his business. Hopefully, if Mary has similar problems, the supervisor is dealing with them. If she is, chances are Dean already knows about it. If Mary is also a problem, and the supervisor is doing nothing, Dean has raised a valid point, and the supervisor had better plan on counseling Mary soon.

Response 3 might be true, but it is off the point. Dean isn't being counseled about his leave balance, but rather his unscheduled use of leave, so the statement proves nothing.

If you believe you are treating everyone the same, get the discussion back to the employee's problem.

You have to be prepared to hear comparisons, but you must avoid getting hooked into the argument. Before you begin the counseling process, you should be thinking about whether you have allowed others to get away with similar behavior. If you have, you deserve to hear about it. If you believe you are treating everyone about the same, get the discussion back to the employee's problem and move on.

Keep Your Objective in Mind; Don't Get Hooked

> *"I know I take a lot of days off, but it's all legitimate. My wife has to be at work at 4 am, so when the kids are sick, I have to stay at home. I can't take them to day care center when they're sick. What do you want me to do, leave a sick kid at home alone?"*

Response 1.

Don't you have relatives who can take care of your kids on occasion?

Response 2.

Why don't you and your wife alternate staying home when the kids are sick? That way, you won't miss so much work.

Response 3.

I understand your situation, just try to do a little better.

Response 4.

I can't tell you what to do. I am telling you there's a problem here at work that I can't live with any longer. You are going to have to make some arrangements to handle these situations.

In a counseling session, you should expect to hear excuses for the behavior in question.

"Last week the battery went dead on my car. I called the auto service, but you know how long it takes them to get to you. It was after noon before they responded, and I have the paperwork to prove it. What would you have done?"

Response 1.

I would have called a neighbor or a taxi and come to work.

Response 2.

If I had so many problems with my car, I would get a new one.

Response 3.

Well, if you have the paperwork, let's just forget about it. But make sure if it happens again, you bring proof.

Response 4.

The issue isn't what you should have done last week. This is about your frequent failures to come to work because of car problems and other things. That must improve.

When you conduct a counseling session, expect to hear excuses for the behavior in question. Also, expect to be asked for your suggestions on how the impossible problems faced by the employee can be solved. Try not to get hooked into either issue. In the two scenarios above, Dean may be presenting valid situations. He may have child care problems and he may have a bad car. Obviously, he is prepared to prove his story about the car. As cold as it may appear, the supervisor is not there to solve his personal problems. She can only try to resolve the work problem.

Don't get hooked into trying to solve an employee's personal problems. You can only try to resolve the work problem.

In both situations, Responses 1 and 2 show the supervisor getting hooked into giving the employee alternatives to resolving his personal problems. These alternatives inevitably will be met with such

The employee should understand that he must handle his personal life in such a way as to meet his work obligations.

responses as *"I tried that and it didn't work out"*, *"That's a good idea, but I can't afford it"* or *"That might work for you, but won't in my situation."* The supervisor's suggestions are no good; therefore, she is failing in her responsibility to help the employee. This is the message you can expect to get, if you allow yourself to get hooked into responding to excuses.

In both situations, Response 3 is inappropriate. This response accepts the excuse. Whether the excuse is valid is not the issue. Dean has not been accused of lying about his need for days off. The problem is the frequency of his unplanned leave. In responding this way, the supervisor allows the discussion to move away from the counseling objective.

Response 4 is proper. Some will view it as cold and uncaring. However, the employee must understand that he has a responsibility to handle his personal life in such a way that he meets his work obligations. That responsibility cannot be assumed by his supervisor. This is not to say that you should never offer suggestions to an employee. If you know of an innovative way someone else has solved a similar problem, by all means, tell him. If you know of a resource available to the employee that might help with his personal situation, make him aware of it.

The supervisor cannot take on the responsibility for the solution to the employee's behavior problem.

You must recognize, however, that the more you get hooked into making suggestions and dealing with the excuses for the behavior, the further you are getting from your counseling objective. Remember, a supervisor's counseling skills are limited. Be careful not to get in over your head.

Make Your Expectations Clear

Never allow an employee to leave the counseling without a clear picture of what improvements to make.

Supervisors often drop the ball at this point. They define and discuss the problem, but they let the employee leave without a clear picture of improvements to make. For some infractions, expectations are obvious. *"I don't want you ever to punch another employee in the nose again"* probably does not need to be said. But for a situation like Dean's, a statement of expectations is necessary.

He has been counseled about taking too many days off without prior notice. Is he never to do it again? How many times can he do it again without incurring the wrath of his supervisor? These are legitimate questions, and the employee deserves some guidance. Dean was told that five days in the past month was unacceptable. How many would be acceptable? Perhaps the supervisor is not in a position to put a number forward. If she were to tell him that two days a month would be about right, you can bet that he will take two days. This may cause additional production problems.

> *"Dean, I recognize that everyone runs into a situation now and then when something comes up and they can't get to work. The problem is, it happens more often than normal to you. I expect the number of instances to decline considerably in your case."*

Is this a fair statement by Dean's supervisor? Should he be entitled to more specific expectations? In this case, it is an adequate statement. For other, more isolated rules violations, a supervisor can be more specific. For ongoing problems like poor attendance, this may be about as specific as the supervisor is able to get. A reasonable person should know what is meant.

Clearly stating expectations should be part of your counseling plan.

It happens more often than normal to you tells him that he should try to conform more to the attendance patterns of his peers. Perhaps if he were to model his behavior after his coworkers, things would be acceptable. This is probably not something a supervisor will come out and say directly to an employee. But there are ways of stating expectations in which you can give indirect messages.

Stating expectations should be part of your counseling plan. Ask yourself before the beginning of the meeting whether your expectations will be obvious from your statement of the problem, or whether you have to go an extra step and state them clearly before you end the meeting. Taking the extra step is usually advisable.

Make the Consequences Clear

Supervisors often are told they can't threaten employees. No such rule appears in the Code of Federal Regulations. However, to remain in compliance with the unwritten rules of supervision, we will deal not with *threats,* but with *consequences.* To reinforce the importance of making a correction, an employee should be told what will happen if his behavior does not change. An employee should know what the supervisor plans as a next step, if one is needed.

An employee should be told what will happen if his behavior does not change.

Do not make idle threats.

In stating the consequences, always remember this: Don't promise something you are unable or unwilling to deliver. If, for example, you say *"If there is one more occurrence of this behavior, you will be suspended for a week,"* hopefully you have checked a few things in advance. Will the agency's table of disciplinary penalties support a week suspension? For state and local governments, will the organization's policies and procedures support the action? Do you have the authority to suspend employees, or must this be done at a higher level? If suspensions are approved at another level, have you discussed the problem at that level to determine whether you will be supported? There is nothing that weakens your counseling efforts more than idle threats.

You must be prepared to do exactly what you have promised, if the employee's behavior does not improve.

It is important, as part of your planning process, that you decide what the next step will be if the behavior doesn't improve. To do this, you may need to talk to your boss to determine whether you will get support. Also, check with your employee relations advisor to determine what the agency usually does with this particular behavior after counseling has not resolved the problem. Then, tell the employee what he can expect if the behavior does not improve.

> *"Dean, if I don't see an immediate improvement, the next step will be to restrict your use of unplanned leave. If that happens, no sick leave will be approved without a doctor's certificate, and no annual leave will be approved unless it is scheduled in advance."*

Now Dean has received clear notice of the consequences of his continued absences. He can now make a choice about whether to work on fixing the problem. He can see how seriously his supervisor views the problem.

Seek a Commitment to Improvement

You won't be successful every time. Perhaps you won't be successful most of the time. However, it is still worth the effort. Toward the end of your meeting, ask the employee whether he understands the problem you have discussed, and why some improvement is needed. If you get a positive response, ask whether he agrees there is a need to change. If he responds in the affirmative, you have some commitment. Don't push your luck and ask him for a signed contract.

Unfortunately, many employees will not be willing to agree openly there is a problem, even though they know better. Some will acknowledge there is a problem, but perhaps not one as serious as you have suggested. Even this is a small victory.

Even without the employee's commitment to improve, you still have the authority to direct it, even if it means resorting to disciplinary action.

Get him to make an effort to change, even if the two of you don't have full agreement on the magnitude of the problem. Some will continue to plead ignorance, despite your presentation of supporting facts. Don't argue any further. So long as you have clearly stated the problem and your expectations, you can live without a commitment from the employee.

When you use the directive approach, getting agreement on the nature of the problem and getting a commitment to improve are bonuses. If it happens, that's great. If it doesn't, you still have the authority to direct improvement, even if that means resorting to disciplinary action. When we look at the use of non-directive counseling to resolve performance problems, we will see that commitment on the part of the employee is absolutely necessary.

CHAPTER SUMMARY

✓ Counseling must be timely. The longer you wait to confront the employee about inappropriate conduct, the less important you make the problem appear.

✓ Avoid counseling the whole workgroup when there are only one or two offenders. Your fear of confronting the responsible individuals only causes you to lose the respect of the entire group.

✓ Get the specific problem out on the table at the opening of the meeting. You are not there to discuss the weather, or to engage in phony praise.

✓ Counseling must be based on facts, not feelings. Be prepared to point out specific examples that caused you to engage in counseling.

✓ Don't let yourself get dragged into a discussion of how you treat others. However, ask yourself before the counseling meeting whether you have confronted other employees who have engaged in similar misconduct.

✓ Avoid getting hooked into advising the employee how to resolve her problems. The more suggestions you give, the more you are taking on the responsibility to solve the problem.

✓ Let the employee know the type of behavior you expect in the future.

✓ Let the employee know the consequences of failing to improve his behavior. Outline the next step if improvement does not occur.

✓ Try to get the employee to commit to improvement.

COUNSELING TO IMPROVE PERFORMANCE

Chapter 6

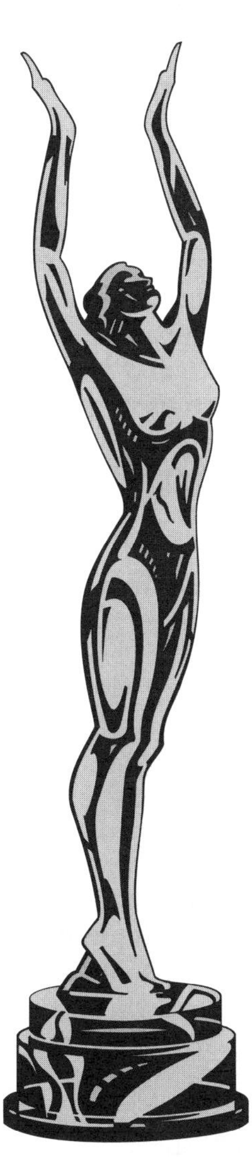

Many people with performance problems want to do a good job.

Assume this and try the non-directive method.

The employee who is not performing up to expectation is a considerably different problem for a supervisor than the employee who refuses to conform to the organization's policies. In this chapter, we will look at counseling techniques you can use to conduct effective non-directive counseling meetings with employees who apparently want to perform well, but are having difficulty meeting performance standards.

There are similarities between the directive and non-directive approaches. You still need a plan and an objective. You must have privacy. You must use facts. You must use clear language. You have to be careful with praise. In reading this chapter, you should keep in mind the points in the previous chapter. The steps used in directive counseling apply also to the non-directive approach. This chapter will deal with the differences between the two approaches, and with the additional skills and techniques you will need to do performance counseling.

Many people with performance problems want to do a good job. It is these people who should be given the benefit of the non-directive approach. If you are certain the employee doesn't care about doing acceptable work, don't waste your time being non-directive. Tell the employee what you want, how to achieve it, and what to expect if she fails to improve. However, if you are dealing with a performance problem, and you aren't sure whether the employee wants to perform well, give her the benefit of the doubt. Assume you are dealing with someone who cares, and try the non-directive method. If she really doesn't want to perform well, it will become apparent soon.

Sometimes, the problem involves a lack of understanding, skill or ability on the employee's part.

One of the reasons performance problems are so difficult to confront is that the employee usually does care. It is not a matter of his being unwilling to follow policies. The problem involves a lack of understanding, skill or ability. The employee behaves properly at work, gets along well with coworkers, and has a good attitude.

The non-directive approach leaves an employee with more positive feelings than the more directive method.

It is much more difficult to confront someone who has all the required characteristics because, as a general rule, you really like the person. This is all the more reason to use non-directive counseling. Instead of telling him what to do, you will be helping him figure things out for himself. This approach leaves an employee with more positive feelings than the more directive method. More importantly, it keeps the responsibility for his performance on his shoulders, where it belongs, and where an otherwise good employee would prefer to have it.

There are challenges to using non-directive counseling. You must be a much more skilled counselor. You must listen well. You must have patience. You must invest more time. Performance problems will not be resolved in one meeting. Even the most well intentioned employees don't often respond to the non-directive method at first. There may be denial that there is a problem. There may be a reluctance to accept responsibility for the solution. Some people, even good employees, like to be told what to do, rather than figure things out for themselves. They believe it is the supervisor's job to resolve all problems.

With non-directive counseling, you must be a much more skilled counselor.

You must listen, have patience and invest more time.

Realize that the non-directive method does not always work to perfection. When you meet resistance, patiently use techniques to keep the counseling flowing in the right direction.

As our example throughout the chapter, we will use Gary, an employee introduced earlier. Gary has performance difficulties, although he has no conduct or attitude problems. His supervisor defined, as her meeting objective for their initial counseling session, the following: *to have Gary identify the possible causes of his poor performance, and to have him outline some steps he will take to improve.* Clearly, the plan is to allow Gary to take the responsibility to identify and resolve his own performance problems. This is the best way to get a lasting solution to which Gary is committed.

Don't give up on non-directive counseling simply because the employee does not begin to discuss his problem.

Unfortunately, things did not go according to plan at thc outset of the counseling meeting. You will remember that Gary's supervisor, using the principle of shared worry, asked him to think about his performance before the meeting. However, when she tried to get him to identify his deficiencies, he denied knowing of any performance problems. She was ready with Plan B, and she outlined problems in two elements of the job—report writing and telephone assistance. She also presented data to back up her conclusions.

Having failed to get the employee to take the ball and begin to discuss his problems, many supervisors would give up and take over the meeting, using directive counseling methods. This is a serious mistake and fails to utilize one of the key abilities needed to be an effective non-directive counselor.

Use Patience and Let the Non-Directive Method Work

For three reasons, supervisors often lack the patience necessary to be successful counselors. First, they are busy. Gary is probably not his supervisor's only problem. She has many other things on her mind, involving both employees and the technical aspects of the work. Second, supervisors are worried. It is unlikely that Gary's performance problems just came to the supervisor's attention. Like most supervisors, she has probably been thinking and worrying about his performance for some months before deciding to talk with him. Finally, supervisors tend to be natural problem solvers. You have exhibited the ability to analyze facts, identify causes and make conclusions.

Remember, don't allow impatience to get in the way of your objective.

These three characteristics add up to impatience. Gary's supervisor has given enough thought to his problems, that she likely has identified for herself the possible causes and solutions. After hearing Gary's reluctance even to admit he has a problem, she is tempted to lay it all out for him. The directive method seems attractive at this point.

Resist the temptation to take over the meeting and become directive.

If she succumbs to the temptation to cut the meeting short by taking over and becoming directive, Gary will leave with a list of possible causes for his problems and several suggested steps he should take to resolve the problems. However, these will not be his ideas; they will have been imposed by his supervisor. If they don't work, and if the performance problems continue, it must be the supervisor's fault for failing to provide the necessary help and advice. This approach will not get the commitment from Gary necessary to achieve a lasting improvement in his performance. Remember that denial of a problem is a natural initial reaction to counseling. She cannot allow impatience to get in the way of her objective.

> Supervisor: *You may not have thought of these as serious problems, Gary, but I have returned several of your reports, and you have been late responding to telephone inquiries. The facts are clear. This doesn't look like acceptable performance to you, does it?*
>
> Gary: *I guess I didn't realize these things were happening so often, but your records show they have. I can't dispute that.*
>
> Supervisor: *Well, now that we agree there is a problem, what do you think might be the causes?*
>
> Gary: *To tell you the truth, I don't have any idea. What do you think?*

Most supervisors would be out of patience at this point. She presented the facts to indicate there is a problem. Gary at least agrees on that point. Now, instead of working on the possible causes, he continues to plead ignorance. Is this the time for the supervisor to switch to the directive approach? Isn't it clear that Gary is not going to cooperate? Without the employee's cooperation, the non-directive method is impossible.

Do not expect denial to go away immediately.

To achieve your objective, you must persist.

Again, she must use patience. What Gary is doing is not uncommon. Even though he is a normally cooperative employee with a good attitude, his competence is being challenged. She must expect that his denial will not go away immediately. To achieve her objective, she must persist.

> Supervisor: *Gary, this meeting is not for me to tell you what your problems are or to dictate solutions. This is to give you a chance to think about why you have these problems and what you might do to fix things. I'm here to help you but not to dictate to you at this time. Maybe it would be best if we took things one element at a time. You are having problems turning in acceptable reports. Think about that element, and what might be the causes of your problems with reports.*
>
> Gary: *Well, I have been thinking about it and...*

Now things have begun to turn in the supervisor's favor. She resisted the temptation to become directive, and insisted that Gary take the ball. She made it easier by focusing his attention on one element of the job at a time. The key is that she refused to give up on her plan.

The non-directive method encourages the employee to express his thoughts and worries.

Notice something in Gary's response. He admits he has been thinking about it. People who aren't doing a good job, particularly those who want to perform well, know it. They may deny it, but they worry about it just as much as the supervisor. The non-directive method encourages them to express their thoughts and worries.

Suppose Gary had not responded appropriately. If he continued to claim he had no idea why he was experiencing problems with his report writing, the supervisor might have done the following.

Sometimes you have to make the non-directive approach work.

> Supervisor: *Gary, I gave you the facts, and we agree you have trouble performing up to standard in two elements of your job. I'm going to stop the meeting now, and we will meet again at 10 o'clock tomorrow morning. At that time, you will let me know what you think is causing these problems, and give me some ideas on what you might do to bring your performance up to standard. Also, let me know how you think I can help. I'll see you tomorrow.*

Sometimes you have to *make* the non-directive method work. That is exactly what she is doing with the above statement. In essence, she is directing the use of the non-directive counseling approach. She knows it is the best way to solve a performance problem, and she is exhibiting the patience necessary to make it happen.

Assume that she has successfully gotten Gary started. He has decided to open up and talk about the problem. Remember, there are two parts to her meeting objective. She wants him to identify possible causes and possible solutions. Now, she must use her non-directive counseling skills to keep him talking on these two points. The following guidelines can help.

Don't Argue

> Gary: *I think there are two things causing my performance to be below standard. I have had several writing courses and quite a bit of experience in writing reports. But the style we use in this office is different from any I've ever used before. We organize our reports differently than anyone I have ever worked for. Also, we are much more wordy in our writing. I was always taught to be concise.*

Don't allow the employee to make excuses for his poor performance. Have him identify causes instead.

> *In responding to our callers in a timely manner, my problem is getting cooperation from the other employees. If we don't share information, we can't respond quickly. For some reason, they don't seem to want anything to do with me. Maybe it's the age difference. I'm over 50 and most of them are in their early 30s. There just doesn't seem to be a connection.*

Gary is making excuses for his poor performance, rather than identifying causes. In one instance, he criticizes the organization's style of writing. In the other case, he blames his performance on his coworkers.

> Supervisor: *Hold on a minute, Gary. We don't encourage poor writing around here. Nor do we organize our reports any differently than any other agency. I've worked for three other agencies, and they all write about the same as we do. Also, I want you to know the other people would never shun you just because of an age difference. They've always been a very cooperative group. I can't agree with your conclusions.*
>
> Gary: *Well, that's the way I see it. Last week, you sent a report back to me in which you added several paragraphs. They just repeated what I had already said. You are just looking for volume. That's not the way I was taught to write.*
>
> Supervisor: *That's not the case at all. You completely failed to explain your recommendations, and I was adding more rationale. I wasn't just adding volume.*
>
> Gary: *Yes, you were.*
>
> Supervisor: *I was not.*

When an employee identifies likely causes and solutions, they do not have to be correct. They only have to be his ideas.

What has just happened to this counseling meeting? She worked so hard to make the session non-directive, and to get Gary's cooperation in resolving the problems. Now, it appears the whole thing has fallen apart. It is the supervisor's fault.

Gary's supervisor has made a critical mistake made by many supervisors who engage in non-directive counseling. Upon hearing his thoughts, she immediately declared him wrong, and went on to defend the organization and the other employees. The meeting now has become an argument, and look who is on the defensive.

It doesn't matter whether Gary's reasons for his poor performance are valid. What matters is he sees things that way. If this is how he feels, he should be given the opportunity to work on solutions. Recognize the employee's performance problems will not be solved in one meeting. Counseling, particularly concerning poor performance, is a *process.* Her meeting objective is to allow him to identify likely causes and solutions. Nothing says they have to be correct. They only have to be *his* ideas.

Do not declare the employee's feelings as wrong. Allow him to work on his ideas.

If she rejects Gary's suggestions, she is becoming directive. She will have to provide ideas of her own. In doing so, she will begin to shoulder the responsibility for improving his performance. To keep that burden on the employee, she must let him work on his ideas. If he is wrong, his performance won't improve, and the burden will remain on him to find some other causes.

This does not suggest that a supervisor should sit silently in a non-directive meeting, accepting anything the employee has to say. However, you must remember some of our previous points about being an effective counselor. Remember, *shut up and listen?*

Remember, shut up and listen?

Remember how important it is to have patience? Now is the time for Gary's supervisor to put some of these suggestions to work. She got him started on the non-directive path. She may not agree with what he has said, but she should let him carry the ball for a while.

Use Questions

Instead of taking a position, and having to defend it, a good non-directive counselor allows the employee to explain and defend his position. The careful use of questions keeps the ball in the employee's court, while requiring him to elaborate on a statement he has made. It is much more effective than arguing whether his statement was correct.

Questions take two forms—those that require a one or two word answer, and those that are open-ended and require some elaboration. Generally, the latter is the better type of question for the non-directive counseling approach.

Assuming Gary's supervisor chose not to argue with him about his suggested causes of his poor performance, and instead used questions, which of the following would be the best question?

The careful use of questions keeps the employee talking... requiring him to elaborate on a statement he has made.

Choice 1.

Which of your coworkers has failed to provide you information when you needed it?

Choice 2.

Don't you think it is your responsibility to ask for the information you need?

Choice 3.

Why do you believe the age differences are a problem?

Arguments are not what the supervisor is looking for.

Regarding Gary's statement concerning his written reports, which would be the best response?

Choice 1.

Which of your reports do you believe I edited without good reason?

Choice 2.

Why didn't you dispute my changes when I gave the reports back to you?

Choice 3.

What are some ways in which your training in report writing and our requirements for written reports differ?

In both cases, Choice 1 is a question that requires a brief response. The question challenges the employee's statement by requiring proof or examples. These are not very effective non-directive questions. They are likely to lead into an argument about whether the employee is correct in his assertions.

Don't argue with the employee's position. Require him to explain it though.

Although stated as questions, Choice 2 in both examples are really arguments. They will again lead directly to a debate about who is right.

Choices 3 are proper non-directive questions. They don't argue with the employee's position. However, they do require him to explain it. He should not feel that the truth of his statement is being challenged. Nor should he feel that the supervisor agrees with what he has said. Rather, he should be encouraged to keep talking about what he believes are the causes of his problems. That is what the supervisor wants at this point in the meeting. When people are given the opportunity to explain, rather than argue about their positions, they are more likely to admit that they may be wrong. Also, if she gives him a chance to elaborate, the supervisor may begin to see that the employee does have a valid point, even though he may not have expressed it well initially.

Mix questions and paraphrases to encourage the employee to go on.

There is nothing wrong with the more direct, pointed question of the *who, what, when* variety. However, in non-directive counseling, you must constantly point toward your objective. If you want the employee to identify causes and plan solutions, you must set the stage for that to happen. Questioning is one way to do that. Your questions should be primarily open ended.

Use Paraphrases

You will drive people crazy if you do nothing but ask questions. Therefore, you want to mix questions with other non-directive techniques, such as the paraphrase. A paraphrase is a concise restatement, but not an exact repeat, of what the employee has said. Its purpose is to indicate that he has been heard and understood. The paraphrase does not indicate agreement or disagreement. It encourages the employee to go on, and lets him know you are listening.

Assume Gary makes the following statement during his counseling meeting.

> *"I don't know what to do. I have taken at least three college courses on writing skills during my career, and I have read a number of books and articles about the subject."*

Paraphrasing does not indicate agreement or disagreement.

Gary's supervisor wants him to keep talking about the problem, but she does not want to develop a pattern of following each statement he makes with a question. She decides to use the paraphrase at this point. Which is the best example?

Choice 1.

You've taken courses and read books.

Choice 2.

Maybe the courses you took were so long ago, you have forgotten the information.

Paraphrasing does not dispute nor agree with what the employee is saying. It only encourages him to continue.

Choice 3.

You have really worked hard on your writing skills.

Choice 4.

Maybe you need to have more training.

Before analyzing the four attempts, we must recognize that paraphrasing is a difficult skill to learn and apply. Supervisors are more used to questioning an employee's statements or to giving suggestions. However, once learned, paraphrasing can be a very effective tool in helping to achieve your non-directive counseling objectives.

Choices 2 and 4 are examples of natural responses to Gary's statement. Rather than paraphrases, they are suggestions. Rather than encourage him to go on with his thought, they take the ball away from him, and give it back to the supervisor. They begin to move the conversation away from the meeting objective.

Choice 1 is a good try, but it is not a paraphrase. Here, the supervisor merely repeats what Gary has already said. Choice 3 is a proper paraphrase. It tells Gary that his point has been heard and understood, and it encourages him to keep talking. His supervisor is not necessarily agreeing that he has made a valiant effort to improve his writing; nor is she disputing that he has worked on his writing. She is only encouraging him to continue.

Assume that later in the counseling meeting, Gary makes the following statement.

"The other people work together on things. They help each other out. I don't have that benefit."

Which would be the best paraphrase?

Paraphrases should be used sparingly and at appropriate places.

Choice 1.

You don't think they like you.

Choice 2.

You don't ask them for help.

Choice 3.

When you run into a problem, you work it out on your own.

All three are admirable attempts at the paraphrase. At least the supervisor is not arguing, questioning or suggesting. Choice 3 is probably the best paraphrase.

Choices 1 and 2 make conclusions that may or may not be accurate. Choice 3 is the most accurate reflection of what Gary said. It doesn't go any further than to indicate he has been heard.

While paraphrases are relatively easy to develop, they are not easy to use. They must be used sparingly and at appropriate places. If you become a paraphrasing fool, it will be apparent you are playing some sort of game, and have the opposite effect from what you intended. Paraphrasing is something you have to practice before you use it seriously. If you are not comfortable with the technique, stick to questions. Just make sure the majority of your questions are open ended. The purpose is to encourage the employee to keep talking and to work toward the objective. The key point to remember is, at this stage of the counseling process, your objective is to let him work things out for himself, with your help.

The key point is to let him work things out for himself, with your help.

Make Effective Use of Silence

Many years ago, psychologists did a study which found that in the average business conversation, neither party will tolerate more than ten seconds of silence.

Use periods of silence to your advantage.

Counseling is a business conversation. If you can be comfortable with a few periods of silence, you can use them to your advantage.

Earlier, Gary and his supervisor were talking about his problems with report writing. Gary was unwilling to admit there was a problem. Another technique his supervisor might have used was silence.

> Supervisor: *Gary, the data is clear. I have had to return five of your last six monthly reports because your conclusions could not be justified. I want you to think about it and tell me what is causing this problem.*
>
> SILENCE
>
> Gary: *I don't really know. I told you I wasn't aware there is a problem.*
>
> MORE SILENCE

The use of silence sends a message to the employee that he is going to have to assume his share of the responsibility.

Try this technique sometime, when talking with someone on a business matter. Count silently to yourself. Rarely will you make it to six. People are uncomfortable with periods of silence, particularly when they know it is their responsibility to keep the conversation going. Gary knows he is having problems with his reports, and he likely has worried about it. The supervisor merely needs to give him the opportunity to express his thoughts. Silence is one effective way to do so. The problem most supervisors have is that they feel responsible for keeping the meeting moving. After all, the supervisor called the meeting. If your objective calls for the non-directive method, you must get over this feeling of responsibility. The strategic use of silence sends a message to the employee that he is going to have to assume his share of the responsibility.

Keep Control

Non-directive counseling does not just allow the employee to wander in any direction he chooses.

At this point, you may be thinking that the non-directive counseling method allows the employee to wander in any direction he chooses. This is not the case. The supervisor must constantly have her objective in mind, and bring the conversation back on track when necessary.

Also, the supervisor has her own ideas about why the employee is performing poorly. Although the non-directive method allows the employee's ideas to be explored thoroughly, it does not prohibit substantial input from the supervisor. Consider the following exchange.

> Supervisor: *Gary, I understand your point about our reports requiring a different style from what you are used to. However, I've noticed that you tend to wait until it gets close to the deadline before beginning to write the report. I wonder if that causes you to rush to get it done, and not think through your conclusions thoroughly.*
>
> Gary: *Maybe you have a point. I do all the research first. But I don't do a draft until my research is completed. Maybe I should be drafting sections of the report at the same time I gather the data.*

Keep control of the meeting without being heavy handed.

Having worried about Gary's report writing, the supervisor has arrived at a few conclusions of her own. She has listened to his ideas about the causes of the problem. She has used questioning and paraphrasing to allow him to elaborate. Now, she introduces some of her ideas. It is likely her ideas will be better received by the employee after he has had a full opportunity to explain his thoughts. She continues to use the non-directive approach, but she makes sure that her points are put on the table for Gary's consideration. She is keeping control of the meeting, without being heavy handed.

Gary has expressed the belief that his coworkers fail to provide him the information he needs to respond to telephone inquiries. Rather than argue with him, the supervisor used open ended questions to

At appropriate times, you should offer observations on the employee's statements.

allow him to fully explain. However, the non-directive method does not require that she merely accept his assertions without presenting her views. At the appropriate time, she might offer the following observation.

> Supervisor: *You know that working with others is a two way street. Are you sure that you are making every effort to communicate with your coworkers, and letting them know the kind of information you need?*
>
> Gary: *I think I am, but maybe it's something I can work harder at.*

There is quite a difference between this exchange and the earlier one in which the supervisor openly disagreed with Gary's feelings about his coworkers. After allowing him full opportunity to explain his feelings, she offers her point of view. He is much more likely to accept the point and agree to work on it, when it is presented in this manner. Again, she is keeping control of the meeting, but in a non-directive manner.

Resist the temptation to save time and dictate the solutions to the problem.

Make the Employee Responsible for Solutions

If the solution is identified by the employee, he will have a greater commitment to success.

After the possible causes of the performance problems have been identified, it is time to identify solutions. Now the supervisor must have the patience to allow the employee to continue to take the lead. There will be a tendency to become directive at this stage. Often, after identifying the causes, solutions are obvious. However, the supervisor must resist the temptation to save time and dictate the steps the employee will follow to resolve the problem. If the meeting has gone on for some time, it might be a good idea to adjourn, and pick up the next day. This will give the employee time to think about his performance improvement plans. It is very important that the non-directive process continue. If the improvement steps are identified by the employee, there will be a much greater commitment to success than if they are dictated by the supervisor.

Improving performance is the employee's responsibility. The supervisor is only the coach.

Supervisor: *Well Gary, now that we have discussed your ideas on what has caused these problems, we should plan what steps you will take to improve. Let's start with the report writing element. You think our organization's writing style is different from the way you've been trained. What can we do to change your style to conform to our expectations?*

Gary: *Obviously, I need different training. Although, I've been to several courses, it has been a few years since I have had training. Maybe some sort of refresher course would work.*

Supervisor: *That's a possibility. What do you have in mind?*

Gary: *I don't know what is available.*

Supervisor: *Why don't you check? Our training office would be a good place to start. They get brochures from various sources. Maybe you ought to make a few calls to training vendors and see what they offer.*

Several important things occurred here. First, the need for training was Gary's idea. It was not dictated by his supervisor. Although training may be an obvious first step, it is important that the employee identify the need. This insures a greater commitment than if the solution came from the supervisor.

Also, the supervisor places the responsibility to find the appropriate training program squarely on his shoulders. Some supervisors would feel it is their responsibility to go to the training office or make the phone calls to find the right course. However, Gary's supervisor is requiring him to do the leg work. In doing so, she is solidifying her message that improving his performance is Gary's responsibility. She is a coach.

An effective coach makes sure the employee is heading in the right direction.

The supervisor will maintain the authority to approve the training. She will probably visit the training office on her own. But it is important that Gary take the main responsibility for finding the right solution.

Giving responsibility to the employee does not mean abdication on the supervisor's part. An effective coach makes sure the employee is heading in the right direction.

> Supervisor: *We agree that, in order for employees to respond to telephone inquiries in a timely manner, they must share information. You think there is a problem with this because of the age difference between you and the others. What ideas do you have to resolve this problem?*
>
> Gary: *I have been thinking a lot about it, and I think we could develop a written form that would facilitate communication. After I get an inquiry, I could summarize it in writing, and give a copy to the person who has the information I need.*
>
> Supervisor: *I don't think a form will solve the problem. We have always dealt with each other in an informal manner. I don't want to change that. A new form would only slow things down.*
>
> Gary: *I don't know what else to suggest, except that I will try harder to communicate with the others when I need information.*
>
> Supervisor: *Why don't you give that a try, and we'll see how it works out. If you make an effort, and we still have a problem, we can look at other possibilities.*

Recognize that counseling is a process and performance problems will not be resolved as the result of one meeting.

Even when the non-directive method works well, and the employee is taking responsibility for solving the problem, he occasionally will come up with an obviously bad idea. Non-directive counseling does not require the supervisor to accept every suggestion. Although you are acting as coach, you have all of your normal decision making authority. In the above example, the supervisor rejected the suggestion of a new form. However, in ruling out the suggested solution, she did not reject Gary's belief that there is a problem between him and his coworkers. She left the door open to further suggestions to resolve that problem.

Gary's supervisor clearly recognizes that counseling is a *process*, and that performance problems will not be resolved as the result of one meeting. Her last statement indicates to Gary that his efforts will be monitored, and that additional discussions will take place.

Establish Specific Plans and Timeframes

It is not enough to agree that the employee will work harder or make more of an effort. You must plan some very specific actions the employee will take to improve his performance. Gary identified a need for additional training in report writing. The supervisor gave him the responsibility to find an appropriate course. She should state this responsibility clearly.

Make a specific plan of action the employee will follow to improve his performance.

Supervisor: *We agree that you will talk with the training officer and identify a course in report writing, along with the course dates and cost. You will do this by next Tuesday, and bring your recommendation to me. You should have a description of the course content and we will discuss how it should help you improve your report writing.*

Gary and his supervisor also made a less specific agreement that he would make more of an effort to communicate his information needs to his coworkers. Even such a general plan can be stated in specific terms.

A specific plan allows for tracking and documenting the efforts that were made.

> Supervisor: *You agree that you will make more of an effort to let the others know when you need information in order to respond to a telephone inquiry. What I would like you to do for the next two weeks is to make a note each time you request information from one of your coworkers, and write down whether and in what time frame the information was given to you. After we review your notes, we will discuss whether we need to plan any further actions in this area.*

You need to be this specific for two reasons. First, the employee must be aware of the steps he is expected to take. There should be no misunderstanding between supervisor and employee about their responsibilities. Also, establishing specific improvement steps allows for better tracking and documentation of the efforts that were made. If, in the long run, performance fails to improve and it becomes necessary to remove the employee from his position, the supervisor will be in a position to prove that she made every effort to assist him.

The employee is responsible for planning solutions that are realistic and within reasonable parameters.

At this stage of the counseling, notice how the supervisor's statements are becoming more directive. This is entirely appropriate. The nondirective method was used to allow the employee to identify the likely causes of his performance problems, and to plan some possible solutions. Now it is time to summarize the agreements that were made, and to insure there is full understanding on what will happen next.

Also, this is the time to let the employee know about the limitations under which you must work. Gary and his supervisor have committed to training as a first step to improve his writing. This does not mean he is free to plan a two week course in the Bahamas. If there are tuition or travel limitations, these must be communicated to the employee. While the supervisor is willing to work with him to improve his performance, Gary must understand that improvement must occur within reasonable parameters. He is responsible for planning solutions that are realistic.

Using the non-directive method will allow you to realize what kind of employee you're dealing with.

Schedule Follow-Up Sessions

Performance improvement rarely happens overnight. An employee who lacks job knowledge or a certain skill or ability will improve incrementally. For this reason, it will be necessary for the supervisor and employee to meet several times to review what improvements have occurred, and plan for additional efforts. In Gary's situation, the two certainly will meet again next week to discuss the training course he identifies. Also, a meeting will have to be scheduled to review the notes he will make regarding his efforts to obtain information from his coworkers. Hopefully, at these meetings, the two parties will be able to identify specific improvements that were made. However, if there is not sufficient improvement, they will have to discuss additional steps that Gary will take to attempt to meet his performance standards.

Earlier, we made the point that the non-directive method is intended for those employees who care about their work, and sincerely want to improve. You will waste your time using non-directive counseling with those employees who don't care about the quality of their work. We suggested that, if you aren't sure whether the employee is sincere, you should give him the benefit of the doubt and use non-directive counseling. When you give the non-directive method a chance to work, and you use some of the techniques described in this chapter, it will become quite obvious to you what kind of employee you are dealing with. Those who care will make a sincere effort to find causes and solutions. Although it may take some initial prodding, they respond well to the non-directive approach.

Those employees who care will make a sincere effort to find causes and solutions.

Employees who don't care about doing a good job, generally won't work with you to explore the causes of their poor performance. They will continue to play dumb or to insist there really isn't a problem. This is your signal to abandon the non-directive approach and begin to dictate your solution to the problem. However, give them a chance to respond. Don't become directive until you have made every effort to let them work things out for themselves.

Don't become directive until you have made every effort to let the employee work things out on his own.

There is no magic formula to tell you how long to go in allowing the employee to plan his own improvement steps. Even the most sincere employee can experience some initial failures. You will have to make a reasonable judgment about when to take over and begin to direct the steps he will take to solve the problem. Just remember that lasting improvement usually must come from within the employee.

Praise, if Praise is Appropriate

In our earlier section, *Be Careful With Praise,* we were critical of how praise is used in counseling meetings, in general. Now we will focus on the proper use of praise in a performance counseling session. Which one of the four options would be the most effective approach for Gary's supervisor to use?

Lasting improvement usually comes from within the employee.

Option 1.

Use no praise until she sees some improvement in his performance.

Option 2.

At the beginning of the counseling meeting: *Gary, I want you to know that generally you do good work.*

Option 3.

Toward the end of the meeting: *Gary, although we have these problems, I want you to know that your performance in other parts of your job is quite good. You are exceeding performance standards in both the Oral Presentation and Research elements.*

Option 4.

Toward the end of the meeting: *You are a valuable member of the team. You're always cooperative. I can count on you to be here when expected, and I know you have a good attitude.*

So long as praise is not used to obscure or lessen the real problem, it is appropriate.

If there are good things that can be said honestly about the employee's performance or behavior, they should be said in the initial counseling meeting. As long as praise is not used to obscure or lessen the real problem, it is appropriate. If he is sincere about improving, he deserves to hear some motivating words. There is no reason for the supervisor to hold out pending noticeable improvement.

Option 2 is the old trick of preparing the employee for the bad news by providing some positive words up front. As discussed earlier, it looks phony and tends to have a negative impact on the discussion.

Options 3 and 4 are both examples of the effective use of praise, assuming, of course, that both are true. Praise is best used toward the end of the meeting, after the problem has been discussed. It allows him to leave with some positive points in his mind, but the problem in no way has been minimized. Option 3 is probably somewhat better than option 4. The purpose of the counseling is to talk about his performance, not his behavior. If the supervisor can point to some positive aspects of his performance, the praise is even more relevant to the discussion.

The most important point about praise, no matter when it is used, is that it must be true. If she is making things up just to make him feel better, he likely is smart enough to figure that out. Then the praise becomes worthless.

Keep Detailed Documentation

We have already discussed the need for documenting every counseling meeting. For performance counseling meetings, your documentation should be more extensive. This is because the non-directive approach covers more ground. If the employee is allowed to identify causes and solutions, the meeting lasts longer and more is said. The agreements made by supervisor and employee need to be documented.

Agreements made by supervisor and employee need to be documented.

Documentation is primarily for the supervisor's protection, even though it is valuable to the employee as well.

Documentation is primarily for the supervisor's protection. It is also valuable to the employee. It provides him a record of the steps he has agreed to follow to improve his performance and it should assist him in tracking his efforts. It is not a bad idea for the supervisor to write a letter to the employee confirming the discussion and the agreements made. This way, both parties are working from the same record, and there will be less chance of a misunderstanding. Documentation of the meeting between Gary and his supervisor might look something like this.

> *We met for one hour on Monday, June 3. I identified poor performance in two of your performance elements—report writing and telephone assistance. I provided examples of instances of poor performance in both elements. In the report writing element, you suggested that our writing requirements were different from those of other organizations for which you have worked. Also, you indicated that your previous training experiences taught a writing style that is different from the one we use.*
>
> *You agreed to attend training to bring your writing into conformance with our expectations. By June 10, you will identify an appropriate training course and discuss it with me. Also, you agreed with my observation that you may be drafting your reports too close to the deadline, causing you to rush through the conclusions. You agreed to write a draft for each section of the report as you complete the research.*

The steps agreed to by the employee for improvement are part of a process that will continue for some time.

There is no requirement that you write a letter to the employee. Your documentation can be kept for yourself. However, performance improvement requires a collaborative process between supervisor and employee. Confirming your agreements in writing should help both parties see where the process is going. It takes extra time, but imagine the time wasted if one of the parties doesn't fully understand the agreement.

CHAPTER SUMMARY

✓ Many employees with performance problems want to perform well, but lack some knowledge or ability. These are prime candidates for the non-directive counseling method.

✓ Non-directive counseling takes more time and patience, and requires higher level counseling skills.

✓ The goal of the non-directive approach is to allow the employee to find the cause of his poor performance and plan solutions. The supervisor acts as a *helper* or *coach.*

✓ Even the most cooperative employees may initially resist the non-directive approach. You must be patient and use counseling techniques that will *let* the non-directive method work.

✓ If you impose your ideas about the causes of poor performance and the possible solutions, you are becoming directive. When this happens, responsibility for performance improvement shifts from the employee's shoulders to yours.

✓ Instead of arguing and directing, supervisors who are skilled at non-directive counseling use techniques such as silence, questioning and paraphrasing to encourage the employee to keep talking and to continue exploring solutions to the performance problem.

✓ Although the employee is given considerable freedom to plan the steps she will take to improve, you should make sure there are specific steps and timeframes established.

✓ You must plan for follow-up meetings to assess progress and plan for more improvement efforts.

✓ Although the non-directive approach places considerable responsibility on the employee, you must maintain firm control over the process. You have final approval over the improvement plan.

✓ People who don't care about the quality of their performance will not respond to the non-directive method. If he doesn't care, it will be obvious quickly.

THE UNUSUAL (HOPEFULLY)

Chapter 7

When an employee states his problems are due to alcoholism, your counseling efforts have just gotten very complicated.

At the beginning of this book, we set out to look at realistic situations. We have avoided bizarre problems, with the intent of dealing with those experiences you are most likely to face. In this chapter, we will look at some situations which are unusual. Hopefully, you will not have to handle these types of problems. Unfortunately, they are becoming all too common.

This section tends to be federal-specific in nature. However, the issues will be similar in state and local governments. Supervisors in non-federal organizations should check specifically with their human resources professionals when applying these issues to their specific circumstances.

What If The Employee Claims To Be Affected By The Use Of Alcohol Or Drugs?

> *"I know my attendance has gotten really bad. I've used up most of my sick leave. I take too many days off for emergencies. I recognize the impact this is having on the work of the unit. But I want you to know it's because of my drinking. Ever since my divorce two years ago, I've been hitting the bottle. I think I am an alcoholic, and I need help."*

If you ever hear a statement like this, your counseling efforts have just gotten very complicated. The employee is claiming his problems are the result of an addiction to alcohol. If it is true that he is an alcoholic, and the disease is causing his poor attendance, he might be entitled to accommodation. You have probably heard plenty about this already. Unfortunately, there are many misunderstandings about the employee's rights in this type of situation. Which response would be most appropriate at this point?

Response 1.

> *If that's your problem, you should go to see our Employee Assistance counselor.*

A supervisor is not qualified to counsel an employee about his addictions.

Response 2.

Whether your use of alcohol is the cause of your attendance problem is not the issue. I am counseling you about your attendance, and that problem must be fixed.

Response 3.

If you are seeking accommodation because of alcoholism, you must prove you have the disability, and you must prove it is causing your attendance problems.

Response 4.

If that's what is causing the problem, you are going to have to make a firm choice between getting immediate help or losing your job.

You may be surprised by this, but all four responses are legally correct. Yet none of them, by itself, is sufficient to convey the proper message.

Since 1981, there have been hundreds of decisions by the Merit Systems Protection Board, the Equal Employment Opportunity Commission and the federal courts concerning the rights and obligations of federal employees who claim an addiction to alcohol. Every agency has an Employee Assistance Program to which such employees can be referred. EAP is an option available to the employee, and generally is not something that can be forced upon the employee. So Response 1 is correct, as far as it goes.

A supervisor is not qualified to counsel employees about their addictions. That sort of counseling is better left to professionals. However, whether an employee is an alcoholic or not, he still is required to come to work. He might be involved in some rehabilitation program, but he must come to work when expected. It is the supervisor's right to continue to counsel him about his attendance, and to take disciplinary action if poor attendance continues. Response 2 is incomplete, but generally correct.

Regardless of the addiction, you have the right to continue to counsel him about his work problem.

An employee disabled by alcoholism is required to get help. Failing to do so can result in losing her job.

Response 3 reflects legal decisions from recent years. An employee who seeks accommodation for a disability must prove that she has the disability and that the disability causes the problems she is having at work. The law was not established to protect casual drinkers who break the organization's rules. It exists to provide accommodation for people who are really disabled by their addiction. The burden of proof is on the person seeking the accommodation.

Response 4 refers to a term called *firm choice*, which has become a term of law in recent years. Now, an employee who is disabled by her alcoholism must be required to get assistance. If she fails to do so, or fails to cooperate in an assistance effort, or if her performance or conduct does not improve, she can be fired.

NOTE: At the time of the writing of this book, the Equal Employment Opportunity Commission issued a new decision in which it indicated that the principle of firm choice will no longer apply to alcoholism cases. It is too early to determine the legal implications of that decision, but it should not change the counseling responsibilities of supervisors.

Things are much more legally complicated than can be described in a few paragraphs. However, this book is about counseling problem employees, and is not intended to be a legal treatise on the alcoholism defense. From the above example, you should get several messages that will impact your counseling efforts, if the employee should raise the alcoholism defense.

First, you have every right to continue to counsel the employee on her performance, attendance and behavior at work. Even employees who are truly addicted have to do their jobs properly. They are not immune from counseling. You should treat them the same way you treat any other employee you counsel. Second, the employee may be entitled to some accommodation. This means he might enroll in an assistance program, and you might have to postpone any planned disciplinary action to give him a chance to be rehabilitated.

Treat the employee with an addiction the same as any other employee.

Seek immediate advice from your employee relations staff when dealing with employee addictions, mental or physical handicaps.

You will have to pay attention to your legal advisors on this. But, keep in mind, your counseling can and should continue, if you are not seeing the changes you expect.

Finally, when an employee raises an issue like alcoholism, drug dependency or any other mental or physical handicap, you must seek immediate advice from your employee relations staff. The law is quite complicated, and supervisors cannot be expected to handle these cases alone. When issues like this are raised, your advisors will probably want to communicate with the employee in writing concerning his rights and obligations. You may be told to postpone further counseling efforts until a letter can be developed. Certainly, you will be advised to continue to monitor the employee's behavior and to document your observations. If you do counsel the employee any further, be sure to document your conversations carefully.

Although the four responses to the employee's statement were, by themselves, legally correct, the more appropriate response would have been something like the following.

> *"If you are an alcoholic, there is help available to you through the agency's EAP or other sources. I will talk to the people in personnel and get advice on how to proceed on that matter. However, I am counseling you about your attendance, and that must begin to improve immediately. You had better begin to make a choice now between your addiction and your job."*

This might appear, on the surface, to be cold and uncaring, but it is the only way to go. You can't try to counsel on the addiction, and you are not a legal expert. The only thing you should continue to talk with the employee about is performance and work behavior. But make sure that you do get that advice from your experts.

If the agency has evidence of a connection between an employee's work problems and use of alcohol or drugs, it is the agency's obligation to raise the issue.

What If You Believe The Problem Is Alcohol Or Drug Related, But The Employee Does Not Raise The Issue In Counseling?

Chances are you think you're off the hook until the employee brings it up. Don't bet on it. Consider this case.

You have supervised Ethel for five years. She is an average employee, with satisfactory ratings, acceptable attendance and works well with others. You know she drinks a lot. She visits the local tavern for lunch just about every day. This does not violate office policy. She does not appear drunk in the afternoon, although she usually has a faint smell of alcohol most of the time. You know she stops at the bar after work every day. She occasionally speaks of hangovers, and, on a few occasions, she has missed work because of hangover.

In the last six months, her attendance and performance have declined considerably. You know it is time to counsel her about this. You have a strong suspicion that the daily drinking is beginning to catch up with her. Which of the following options would be most appropriate at some point during the counseling meeting?

Option 1.

Speak only about the performance and attendance. Say nothing about her drinking unless she brings it up.

Option 2.

Ethel, it is very important that you not allow outside influences, such as drinking, to affect your work.

Option 3.

Sometimes these types of problems are caused by something going on in one's personal life. Things like marital problems, money problems, or alcohol use. I have no evidence that this is happening to you, but if there is something like this causing these problems, I want to make you aware of our employee assistance program.

Confrontation may seem harsh and direct, but it is necessary.

Option 4.

Ethel, I have observed that you drink almost every workday. Also, you have mentioned not being able to come to work because of hangover. I think your drinking could be the cause of these problems. If it is, I want you to get help.

Although Option 1 is very attractive, and even somewhat logical, you must rule it out. The legal authorities who decide these cases, have made it clear that, if the agency has evidence there may be a connection between an employee's problems at work and her use of alcohol, it is the agency's obligation to raise the issue. This is the first step in providing the reasonable accommodation the law requires. If the agency has evidence and fails to confront the employee with it, then later fires the employee for her poor work or attendance, and the employee raises the alcoholism defense at the last minute, the agency likely will lose the case. On the other hand, if the agency confronts the employee with the evidence, and the employee fails to take advantage of the opportunity to accept assistance, the agency will be in a much better position to defend a disciplinary action if one becomes necessary.

At this point, you are probably saying that the agency has no proof Ethel's problems are caused by her drinking. It may not have proof, but it does have evidence. A supervisor's observations constitute evidence. Legally, the evidence should be presented to Ethel.

Options 2, 3 and 4 constitute a supervisor's attempts to confront Ethel with his suspicions. All are admirable, but only one is sufficient. Option 2 mirrors a supervisor's counseling attempt in a case that was decided by the Merit Systems Protection Board in 1981. The Board found this statement a weak attempt at confrontation that failed to meet the requirements of law.

Option 3 is better, but not quite good enough. It hints at the supervisor's suspicions, but falls short of the necessary confrontation. As harsh and direct as it appears, Option 4 is the correct way to approach Ethel, both from a legal and practical point of view.

When confronted directly about an addiction, the employee cannot later argue that she did not understand.

In Option 4, the supervisor doesn't accuse Ethel or diagnose her as an alcoholic. However, he does directly state his observations. She is likely to react angrily. However, in order to prove later that Ethel was given an opportunity at accommodation, the agency must prove that she was directly confronted with the supervisor's suspicions. She is free to deny it, but she cannot later argue that she didn't understand.

Experts on alcoholism would support Option 4 over the other statements. They have learned that dancing around the problem or hinting at it does not affect an alcoholic. Denial is the alcoholic's first reaction. Direct confrontation is the only way to approach the problem.

Of course, carefully documenting the discussion is necessary. It would be wise for the supervisor to write as exactly as possible what he said to Ethel concerning her drinking. If a disciplinary action later becomes necessary, the supervisor's handling of the initial confrontation could be very important to winning the case.

What Happens If The Employee Threatens Violence?

It is quite unfortunate to have to deal with this issue. However, while this book was being written, there were three news accounts involving people being killed by disgruntled coworkers. The first thing every supervisor should do is read some books or get some training on workplace violence. The problem has become so pervasive that new books and courses are appearing on the market regularly.

Never take any threatening statement lightly.

You cannot take any threatening statement lightly.

> *"I can understand why some employees go off the deep end and come in shooting."*

If this statement were made by an employee during a counseling meeting, would it constitute a threat? From a legal perspective, for the purpose of initiating disciplinary action, it would depend on a number of factors. Did the person who heard the statement fear harm?

Many organizations have formed teams to analyze and react to threatening statements.

In what context was it made? These are the types of questions the Merit Systems Protection Board and the courts will ask.

As the employee's supervisor, you cannot ignore it. You should report it to your manager, and you should discuss it with your employee relations advisors. Many organizations have formed teams to analyze and react to statements like these.

At the counseling meeting, upon hearing such a statement, your response should be to ask for clarification. *What do you mean by that? Why do you feel that way?* These questions will help you determine whether the statement was made in jest or whether the employee is expressing some real feelings. Also, if the situation is not too volatile, it would be appropriate to remind the employee that such statements, even said in jest, are not acceptable at the workplace. Even if you determine that the statement was not meant as a threat, you should discuss it with other members of management to determine whether further action is warranted.

If there is any possibility of violence, you should not meet alone with an employee.

If there is any possibility of violence, you should not meet alone with an employee. If the immediate supervisor is a source of irritation to an employee who has expressed violent tendencies, counseling should be done by other levels of management.

During a counseling meeting, if you begin to fear a violent reaction, there are several immediate measures you can take. Keep your voice quiet and as calm as possible. Don't get into a shouting match. Give the employee plenty of physical space. Silence and paraphrasing are recommended by violence experts as calming influences. Allow the employee to explain his dissatisfactions, but make sure he understands the type of behavior you expect. Don't hesitate to have security personnel nearby if you anticipate trouble.

Don't hesitate to have security nearby if you anticipate trouble.

How Do You Handle Threats of Grievance, Complaints and Lawsuits?

Go back a few pages to the supervisor's counseling of Ethel, the employee whose problems might be caused by her drinking. Suppose the supervisor did make the statement in Option 4, which was the proper statement to make.

Ethel reacts as follows.

> *"You have no right to call me an alcoholic. I'm contacting my attorney and I intend to file a slander suit immediately, along with a grievance and an EEO complaint."*

What would be the most appropriate reaction by the supervisor?

Choice 1.

Hold on a minute Ethel, you can be disciplined for making threats like that. I don't have to put up with this.

Choice 2.

Ethel, you don't know what slander is. I can't be guilty of slander. I didn't make the statement publicly. I just expressed my personal opinion privately to you.

Choice 3.

Ethel, I didn't call you an alcoholic. I told you what I've observed and my opinion that your drinking could be a cause of your work problems. If you feel the need to contact an attorney, that's your right. And you have the right to use the grievance or EEO procedures if you think I have done something wrong.

Choice 4.

Go ahead and file. See where it gets you. If you want trouble you will get it.

An employee has the right to call a lawyer and file a complaint. Never threaten an employee for wanting to do so.

This was an easy one. Choices 1 and 4 suggest retaliation against the employee if she exercises or threatens to exercise her legal rights. She has the right to call a lawyer and file a complaint. If she is threatened for doing so, the supervisor has brought much trouble upon himself.

Choice 2 argues the merits of a potential lawsuit. It detracts from the counseling objective, wastes time and promises not to resolve anything.

Choice 3 is the only appropriate response. The supervisor briefly explains his statement, and acknowledges Ethel's legal right to do what she has threatened. There really is no other way to react. You cannot back off because of a threatened complaint. If you are doing your counseling properly, you have nothing to fear.

Some employees pay a lawyer to call or visit the supervisor to make such threats. Lawyers can be awfully intimidating. However, your response to a threat from a lawyer should be no different than the suggested response to Ethel. Lawyers like to use a tactic in which they accuse you of violating *"the law"* or *"her rights."* The best response is to ask calmly *"what law (or right) did I violate, and how did I commit such a violation?"*

If you are counseling properly, you have nothing to fear from an employee threatening to file a complaint.

CHAPTER SUMMARY

✓ If an employee raises substance abuse as a defense for his performance or conduct problems, you should consult with your human resources advisor promptly. The employee may be referred to your Employee Assistance Program. However, you have the right to expect improvement in the performance or conduct that led to the counseling.

✓ If you suspect alcohol abuse is causing an employee's problems at work, you have an obligation to confront her with your suspicions. Talk with your human resources advisor before initiating such a discussion.

✓ Threatening statements never should be ignored, even if said in apparent jest. Many organizations have formed teams of managers and specialists to analyze such statements and to decide how to approach the employee.

✓ People have the right to file grievances and complaints over anything you do. Don't let threats of complaints stop you from doing your job.

A SUMMARY CHECKLIST

Chapter 8

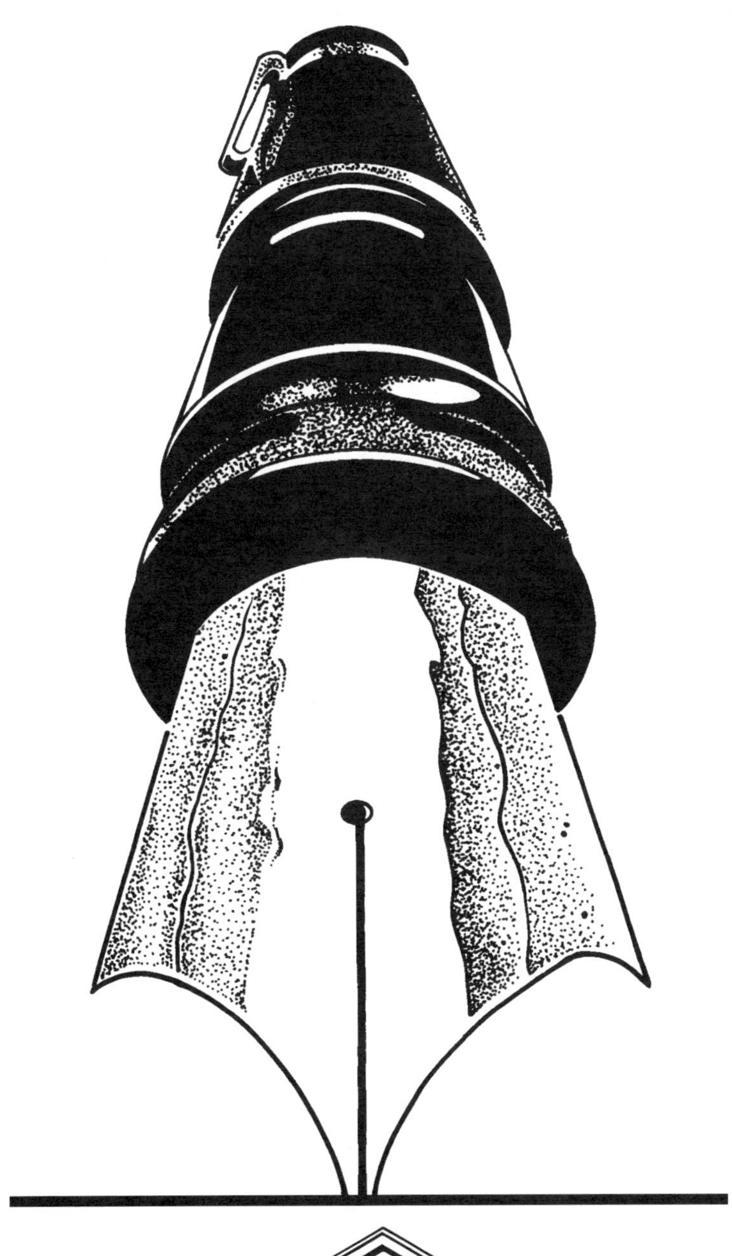

Remember, there is no magic to identifying the need for counseling.

Many points have been made in the preceding pages. The purpose of this final chapter is to put everything in order. What follows are the steps you should go through after you have determined there is a need to confront a problem employee. Remember, there is no magic to identifying the need for counseling. It is a feeling you get in the pit of your stomach. Our checklist begins soon after you get that feeling.

✓ Pinpoint the Problem

What is really bothering you about this employee? You must nail this down as specifically as you can if your counseling is to be successful. You have seen what happens if the supervisor fails to correctly identify the problem at the outset of the counseling meeting.

What is really bothering you about this employee?

Maybe it is something about his attitude that bothers you. That's not going to be good enough. What behaviors are you observing that cause you to question his attitude? Is he argumentative? Does he fail to pitch in and help when things get busy? If you can't identify specific instances of unacceptable behavior or performance, it is probably not time to counsel. Remember that many employees act surprised when initially counseled. They tend to deny knowledge of any problem. The only way to overcome this is with examples. Gathering this type of data is a necessary prelude to counseling.

Try writing a problem statement for your own use.

Try writing a problem statement, just for your own use. Then ask yourself whether it makes sense, or does it evoke the response *"So what?"* Consider this example.

> *Mary has been a government employee for 20 years, and has a sick leave balance of only 40 hours.*

There is no problem stated here, at least as far as the supervisor is concerned. There is no rule requiring any employee to maintain a certain leave balance. What you must do is write down what about Mary's behavior is really bothering you. Perhaps she wasn't at work two days this week when you badly needed her.

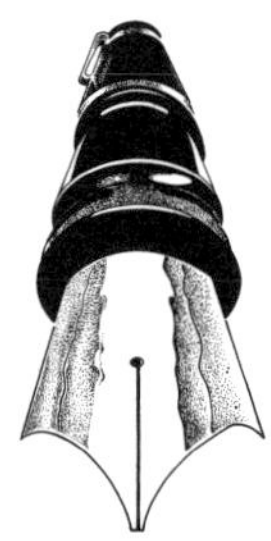

Gather facts and then determine what bothers you about those facts.

Maybe she takes a lot of sick days when things get busy. Gather some facts, then determine what about those facts troubles you. Chances are the real problem is something like this.

> *Mary uses a lot of sick leave in one or two day increments, and it really disrupts our operation.*

Now you will be prepared to begin your counseling on the right track.

Identify whether you are dealing with a performance or a behavioral problem.

In identifying the problem, there is one other important concern you must address. That is whether you are dealing with a performance or behavioral problem. This decision sometimes will be easy. If George punches another employee, he clearly has behaved improperly. However, if Mary turns in a bad work product, is it because she lacks some knowledge or skill? Could it be that she didn't want to do the assignment in the first place? Is it because she was off two days on sick leave?

Before you begin to counsel, you must try to make this decision. Sometimes it won't be possible. By now, you know that performance problems require a different counseling approach than behavioral problems. You must decide whether you are dealing with someone who *can't* do the work, or someone who *won't* do what is expected.

✓ Gather Supporting Facts

Plenty has been said about this already, so this section will be brief. Remember to be prepared for the ignorance defense. You are identifying a need for counseling, so the burden is upon you to prove that need. *"You have been using a lot of leave"* is a very weak statement, if challenged. *"You have used five days of unplanned annual leave and three days of sick leave during the past month"* is much more concrete.

Part of fact gathering is determining how the employee's performance or conduct affects or has the potential for affecting the organization.

It's much easier to begin counseling with facts in hand.

"Your approach turns people off" doesn't say much. *"I have had three complaints from people about how abrasive you are when they ask you for information"* gives so much more to work with.

Facts like these are not always available, but you should seek them out. It is much easier to begin counseling with facts rather than feelings.

✓ Develop Your Plan

A whole chapter has been devoted to planning. It is the key to combating fear. You must develop an objective, but remember to make it a *meeting objective.* Of course, you're counseling to bring about a change in behavior or performance, but that may not happen overnight. So write down your objective for the specific counseling session you are about to conduct. Once you have an objective, you have a much better chance of keeping the session on track. If you don't know where you want to go, it will be difficult to maintain control.

A plan with a meeting objective is imperative. If you don't know where you want to go, it will be difficult to maintain control of the counseling meeting.

Your objective will lead you to a decision about whether you want to use the directive or non-directive approach. Also, develop Plan B just in case the employee does not respond as you anticipate. If things don't go according to plan, don't abandon your plan too quickly. Counseling requires patience.

Finally, keep in mind the importance of having an opening statement that specifically defines the problem. You are not there to talk about the weather or some sporting event. Nor have you scheduled the session to heap praise upon the employee. State the purpose and get down to business.

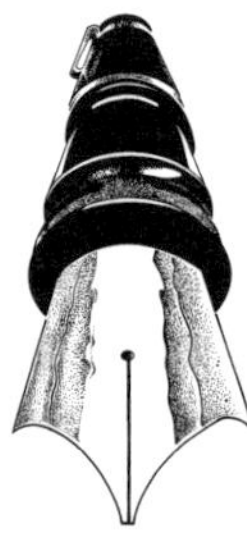

✓ Schedule With the Employee in Advance

Scheduling with an employee alllows him to prepare and makes the process more efficient.

Apply the principle of shared worry. It may appear to be a cruel game, but there is more to it than that. The element of surprise is rarely effective. If an employee hasn't had advance notice of the counseling, you are more open to the claim of ignorance. Employees should be prepared for counseling. It makes the process more efficient. However, recognize that you had better be well prepared also. There really is nothing wrong with making a problem employee do a little worrying. You certainly have to do plenty.

✓ Find the Time and a Proper Place

If you are going to do performance counseling, plan on spending more time than you will for behavioral counseling. One of the best conversation stoppers is for one of the parties to be glancing at his watch, because he has something else scheduled. Don't start looking for a meeting room ten minutes before the session. You won't achieve your objective if you have to worry about adequate privacy or if you have to rush.

✓ Do It

Don't put off dealing with a problem.

You know the problem. You are ready to prove there is a problem. You have an objective and a plan. Do yourself a favor, and don't put it off any longer. Practice some of the techniques discussed in previous chapters, and use them. They work. Keep in mind, it is your meeting and you are in control. If the employee brings an unexpected representative, don't feel guilty about postponing to talk to your advisor. If she refuses to cooperate with the non-directive approach, you may want to schedule another session to give her time to think about it.

Evaluate your performance so you can improve each time you conduct a counseling meeting.

Use the non-verbal listening techniques discussed earlier. Allow the employee to have full input, but make sure your objective is always kept clearly in sight.

Whether you are using the directive or non-directive approach, your counseling meeting should accomplish three things. When the meeting ends, the employee should understand the problem, know your expectations, and know the consequences or the next step.

After the counseling meeting, take some time and evaluate your performance. You won't become an expert at this quickly. There always will be something you wish you had or had not said. Try to improve each time you conduct a counseling meeting.

✓ Plan for Follow-Up

Name a date, time and place for your follow-up meeting. Be specific.

If you counsel to improve performance, the employee should leave the meeting with some specific actions for which she is responsible. You should schedule a meeting to review those actions in the near future. Don't say *"We will discuss this again soon."* The correct approach is *"Tuesday, June 17, we will meet at 9 am to talk about what you have accomplished on the three actions you have agreed to take."*

When you are counseling to correct an employee's conduct, a specific follow-up meeting may not be necessary. You may be in a situation in which he will either commit the offense again, or clean up his act. Follow-up will depend upon what happens after the counseling. However, if you feel the employee is not committed to changing, or doesn't seem to understand why he should change, don't hesitate to schedule another meeting. Consider this approach.

> Supervisor: *We've talked about the need for you to cut back on the long lunches. We need you here to handle phone calls, and we can't have others constantly making excuses for you. Do you understand this?*

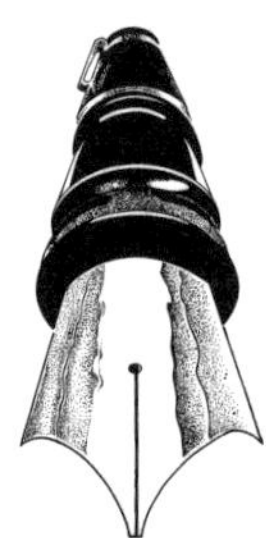

A follow-up session is a tool to impress upon the employee the importance for change.

Employee: *I think you're overreacting. I will do what you want, but I don't agree with it. What is important is that I give out the proper information to callers, not that I'm there when they call.*

Supervisor: *Well, we disagree on that point. What I am going to do is keep an eye on things for the next month. Then one month from today, on the fifteenth, we will meet at 2 pm to see whether things have improved. Put it on your calendar.*

What the supervisor faced here was a very reluctant commitment. The employee agreed to change his behavior, but failed to see a reason to do so. This is a counseling meeting that cries out for a scheduled follow-up. The employee is quite likely not to make a lasting change if he disagrees with the need for the change. So it is probable more discussion will be needed. A follow-up session is scheduled in this case to impress upon the employee the importance the supervisor places on the need for change. You can't reach across the table and grab him by the throat until he makes the commitment you seek. But you can make your point by scheduling a follow-up meeting.

Planning a follow-up does not mean the two of you won't discuss the problem sooner. If he takes another long lunch tomorrow, get him back in there. Don't wait for the scheduled meeting.

✓ Prepare Your Documentation

We have seen that documentation can be relatively simple, or in performance counseling, somewhat more complex. All documentation should contain the date of the meeting, the names of those present, and the matters discussed. Make sure it shows your stated purpose of the meeting, and your statement of the problem. It should summarize the employee's reaction, and any commitments or agreements made by the employee.

Remember, documenting counseling sessions enables you to show the employee understood your expectations.

Finally, it should show that you discussed the consequences or the next step that would occur. Whether you give a copy to the employee will depend upon your own preference, your organization's policy, and your union contract, if there is one. There is no legal requirement that the employee be given a copy of your notes. You can choose to confirm the counseling with a letter summarizing the meeting. However, this is not a necessary step.

If problems persist, your documentation of subsequent counseling meetings should get more detailed. If you are not seeing the changes you expect, and you continue to counsel, you probably should begin to confirm the results of your meetings in a letter to the employee. It is beginning to look like disciplinary action will occur, and you don't want him to be able to successfully argue that he didn't understand your expectations.

Don't change your behavior after a counseling session.

✓ Resume Business As Usual

Of course, things may be a little tense for a while. Some employees brood for some time after counseling. If coworkers know an employee was counseled, there can be some discomfort throughout the whole work unit. You will be keeping a close eye on the employee to determine whether she will begin to make the changes you expect. Hopefully, you won't see the need to follow her around, observing her every move.

This was mentioned earlier, but deserves some emphasis. Don't lock yourself in your office until the period of discomfort subsides. Try to deal with everyone, including the counseled employee, the way you always have. If you usually have a Monday morning meeting, don't change. If you borrow the counseled employee's newspaper every day at lunch, keep doing it.

Allow everyone to see that you are prepared to correct problems without turning them into emergencies.

The message you are giving is that there is a problem being tackled, but that you or the organization have not changed as a result. This allows everyone to see that you are prepared to correct problems without turning them into emergencies.

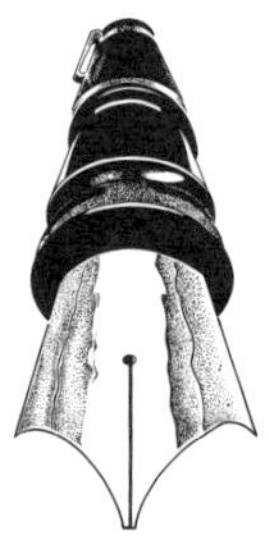

By not avoiding the employee, it reinforces the principle of attacking the problem, not the individual.

It allows the problem employee to see that his status in the organization remains intact, and will continue, so long as he makes the change you expect. It reinforces the principle of attacking the problem, not the individual.

✓ Determine Whether You Will Get Support

This does not necessarily belong as the last point on our checklist. It will be up to your judgment as to when to take this step. Some will want to do it before they ever begin to counsel an employee. Others will wait until they see whether their initial counseling efforts have any impact. Whatever you choose, at some point in the counseling process this step should be considered.

You have a right to know whether the organization will support you if you take on a problem employee.

The first sentence of this book defined supervision as the hardest job there is. It was sincerely meant. Unfortunately, supervision, particularly in government agencies, seems to be getting even harder. In recent years, someone decided there were too many supervisors and you became the target of cutbacks. We now hear that you should be able to supervise 15 employees, instead of the traditional seven or eight. We hear about organizations using the team concept where people have the title leader rather than *supervisor.* We don't quite understand how this changes traditional supervisory responsibilities. We don't know who is expected to counsel the problem employees. Chances are, it will continue to fall on your shoulders. It probably won't be done by the team.

Unfortunately, many organizations are very reluctant to take actions against problem employees. They fear the complaints and court battles that may follow. Some organizations don't want to challenge even their worst employees, fearing adverse publicity, although they know they can win an appeal. Managers continue to look to supervisors to handle problems at the lowest level. However, you have a right to know whether, and to what degree the organization will support you if you take on a problem employee.

Keep the higher levels of the organization informed about problems.

It always has been the practice of supervisors to keep the higher levels of the organization informed about problems. Today, it has become more important to do so, and to do it early. If you are planning to confront an employee about his performance or conduct, it might be a good idea to have a meeting with your boss first, and let her review your counseling objective and plan. Unfortunately, some employees have learned that, after they have a confrontation with their immediate supervisor, they need only visit the manager one or two levels above to find a sympathetic ear. If this is going to happen after you have gone through the pain of preparing for and conducting a counseling meeting, the process isn't worth it.

If you work in an organization in which managers support the correct efforts of their supervisors, you still need to keep the higher levels informed as you go through the process. When you counsel someone, you should clearly state the consequences of failure to make the necessary changes. As was mentioned earlier, you must avoid idle threats. If you are going to tell someone he will be disciplined for one more instance of misconduct, you must check not only with your line managers, but also with your staff advisors, to determine whether the organization will allow you to follow through.

Don't hesitate to go up the management chain for a review of your objectives and plans.

Counseling is effective. The large majority of employees want to do well. Some of them need guidance from their supervisors in the form of periodic counseling meetings to remind them of expectations, or to work on performance deficiencies. Most employees will respond positively to the counseling steps and techniques outlined in this book. However, there are a few employees who will push things as far as they can because they think you are afraid to confront them. You might not fear such confrontation. You might even think it is your duty to the employee's coworkers and to the taxpayer. But when you know you are about to do battle with one of these people, you must also think of yourself. Don't hesitate to go up the management chain and let your objectives and plans be reviewed. Find out if the organization is willing to support your efforts to bring about the kind of performance and conduct expected of government employees.

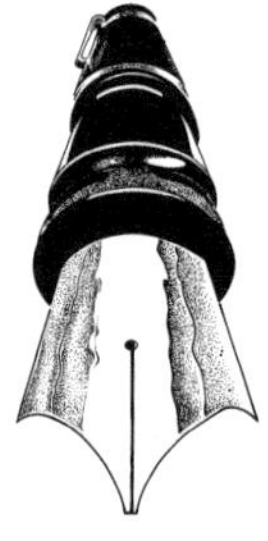

Be mindful of the value of letting people know when things are going well, not just when there is a problem.

As promised at the outset, this book has been about dealing with problems. Hopefully, you recognize that problem employees constitute a small percentage of the workforce. You must also recognize the percentage has a tendency to grow if the problems are not tackled.

You should be mindful of the value of letting people know when things are going well, not just when there is a problem. There is nothing wrong with taking a minute to stop at someone's desk to tell him you really liked the job he did last week on a special project. Then, if it ever becomes necessary to correct that same employee's behavior, you won't have to make up some phony praise. He will remember the praise he got at the time it was due. If you have to counsel someone about a problem, which of the following statements would you prefer truthfully to be able to make?

Option 1.

Jack, before we get started, I want to tell you what a good job I think you are doing, but there is one problem we must deal with.

Option 2.

Jack, despite the problem we have had to discuss, I hope you remember the number of times I have been able to tell you what a good job you did.

Another easy one.

FPMI Publications

FPMI Publications

Alternative Dispute Resolution: A Program Guide
Building the Optimum Organization for Federal Agencies (2nd Edition)
Career Transition: A Guide for Federal Employees
Customer Service in the Government
Diversity: Straight Talk From the Trenches
EEO Settlements Through Interest-Based Resolutions
Face to Face: A Guide for Supervisors Who Counsel Problem Employees
Federal Employee's Guide to EEO (2nd Edition)
Federal Manager's Guide to Discipline (4th Edition)
Federal Manager's Guide to EEO (4th Edition)
Federal Manager's Guide to Improving Employee Performance
Federal Manager's Guide to Liability (2nd Edition)
For Official Use Only: Managing Cyberspace in the Workplace
How to Build an Effective Team
HR Guide to Managing Organization Change
Managing Diversity: A Practical Guide
Managing Diversity in the New Reality
Managing Effectively in a Reinvented Government (2nd Edition)
Managing Leave and Attendance Problems (5th Edition)
Managing the Civilian Work Force (3rd Edition)
Measuring Organizational Performance
Performance Management: Performance Standards and You
Practical Guide to Interest-Based Bargaining (2nd Edition)
Practical Guide to Self-Managed Teams
Practical Ethics for the Federal Employee (3rd Edition)
RIF and the Federal Employee (2nd Edition)
Sexual Harassment and The Employee (4th Edition)
Supervisor's Guide to Federal Labor Relations (5th Edition)
Understanding Employee and Family Friendly Leave Policies
Understanding the Federal Retirement Systems (3rd Edition)
The Union Representative's Guide to Federal Labor Relations (2nd Edition)
Ways of Wills (4th Edition)
Working Together: A Practical Guide to Labor-Management Partnerships
You're In the Unit Now

Practitioner Publications

Desktop Guide to Unfair Labor Practices
The Federal Employment Law Practitioner's Handbook
Workplace Harassment: A Practitioner's Guide

FPMI Newsletters

FedNews OnLine™ (a free daily e-newsletter covering federal issues and concerns. Get it! www.fpmi.com)
The Federal Labor & Employee Relations Update
The MSPB Alert
The EEO Update
The Federal HR Edge

FPMI's e-Packages

The e-Fed™ e-Package
The e-Fed™ e-Package is a multiple-newsletter Internet-based research service. The package includes the FedProHR™ e-Package and its research systems that search full-text decisions and case summaries of the FLRA and MSPB decisions, the EEO Update and the Federal HR Edge.
The package is affordably designed to provide agencies the tools needed in the Labor and Employee Relations, Human Resources and EEO arenas. This comprehensive package includes all FPMI newsletters and research services.

FPMI Publications

FedProHR™ e-Package
The FedProHR™ e-Package is a multiple-newsletter Internet-based research service. The package includes three newsletters, The MSPB Alert, The LER Update and The FLRA Bulletin and its research systems that search full-text decisions and case summaries of the FLRA and MSPB decisions.

EEO Update e-Package
The EEO Update e-Package is an Internet-based newsletter that provides access to summaries of significant EEO case decisions as well as significant news and features on EEO events occurring in the federal government.

Federal HR Edge e-Package
The Federal HR Edge e-Package is an Internet-based service that provides access to news and events affecting all federal employees and supervisors.

Federal Labor & Employee Relations Update e-Package
The Federal Labor & Employee Relations Update e-Package is an Internet-based service that provides articles, full-text decisions, case summaries and key points of the most significant FLRA, FSIP and MSPB cases each month.

MSPB Alert e-Package
The MSPB Alert e-Package is an Internet-based research service that provides access to summaries and full text decisions of decisions issued by the MSPB.

All packages are sold through an affordable annual license that provides an agency unlimited access to this Internet service. Visit the FPMI web site at http://www.fpmi.com for more information.

Training
FPMI Communications, Inc. specializes in training seminars for federal employees, managers and supervisors. These seminars are offered as scheduled open enrollment classes or they can be conducted at your worksite at a flat rate.

The instructors for FPMI seminars have all had practical experience with the federal government and know problems federal supervisors and employees face and how to deal effectively with those problems.

TASK Force™
FPMI offers consulting and technical assistance services to federal agencies in all aspects of human resources, management and EEO. With our extensive network of consultants we are ready to assist you by providing experienced professionals to perform specific tasks in virtually any human resources field, from labor relations to position classification. If you need temporary or long term assistance, we can provide you immediate expert assistance. Call FPMI to learn more about subjects covered, satisfied customers, and pricing.

For your convenience, you may order FPMI's products and services off the GSA Federal Supply Schedule and avoid expensive and time consuming agency procurement processes.

For more information on our products and for pricing contact:
FPMI Communications, Inc.
707 Fiber Street, Huntsville, AL 35801-5833
PHONE (256) 539-1850, FAX (256) 539-0911
Email: fpmi@fpmi.com; Internet: http://www.fpmi.com